Promised Land

Other Books by Glenn Alan Cheney

Love and Death in the Kingdom of Swaziland

*How a Nation Grieves: Press Accounts of the Death of Lincoln,
the Hunt for Booth, and America in Mourning*

Thanksgiving: The Pilgrims' First Year in America

*Journey on the Estrada Real:
Encounters in the Mountains of Brazil*

Journey to Chernobyl: Encounters in a Radioactive Zone

Frankenstein on the Cusp of Something

Passion in an Improper Place

*They Never Knew: The Victims of Atomic Testing
Acts of Ineffable Love: Stories by Glenn Cheney*

Acts of Ineffable Love

Promised Land

A Nun's Struggle to Resist
Landlessness, Lawlessness, Slavery, Poverty,
Corruption, Injustice, and Environmental Devastation
in Amazonia

Glenn Alan Cheney

New London Librarium

Promised Land: A Nun's Struggle to Resist Landlessness, Lawlessness, Slavery, Poverty, Corruption, Injustice, and Environmental Devastation in Amazonia

Parts of this book originally appeared as an article in the June 2013 issue of *Harper's Magazine*.

Photos in this book can be seen in color in the eBook edition. Photographs are by Glenn Alan Cheney except for the one depicted in the reproduction of the first page of the *Harper's* article, taken by Nadia Shira Cohen.

Published by   in cooperation with
New London Librarium   Fogão de Lenda
18 Parkwood Rd.   CP 3173 - Savassi
P.O. Box 284   Belo Horizonte, MG
Hanover, CT 06350   30130-972
USA   Brazil
www.NLLibrarium.com   www.fogaodelenda.com

ISBN
978-0-9856284-6-8 [paperback]
978-0-9856284-7-5 [eBook]

Contents

Promised Land

Glenn Alan Cheney

Chapter One

Pistoleiros

I'm sitting in the back seat thinking, *nuns can't drive.* Or maybe it's just nuns with a lot on their minds. Or maybe it's just Sister Leonora, bearing on her sixty-four-year-old shoulders the weight of slavery, kleptocracy, landlessness, lawlessness, forest fires, hit squads, environmental devastation, and the ravages of capitalism. The year is 2010 and she's driving erratically down a ragged highway in the central Brazilian state of Mato Grosso, just south of a state called Amazonas. She speeds up, slacks off, squints into the dark beyond the headlights, then remembers the rearview mirror, then remembers the accelerator.

Half the problem, I think, is the woman sitting next to her,

Elizete. She's telling a florid, multi-faceted tale of political shenanigans at town hall in Terra Nova do Norte. She works there, a sub-secretary of environmental issues, knee-deep in a political slurry of "detoured" money. She hates it. As she tells her tale of atrocities, her voice soars and sings with emotional involvement. I'd have trouble driving, too.

Then Leonora stops her with a finger tapping the rearview mirror. "They're following us," she says.

"Who?" Elizete asks.

"*Pistoleiros.*"

No matter how fast she goes, she says, they stay a few hundred meters behind, never closer, never farther. They've been with us since we filled the tank back in Alta Floresta, half an hour ago. She was pretty sure she recognized them back there, the car anyway. We're still an hour from the next town. Between here and there the houses are few, cars rare, the sky more than dark with the smoke of burning pastures and the scant patches of forest that remain in this part of Amazonia. It's a good place for a hit. There's no cell phone signal, but that matters little since there's no one to call. Certainly not the police. The guys in the car behind us are probably police, off duty for the moment. Leonora says, "If there's a police block up ahead, you two take care of yourselves. Don't worry about me."

Take care of ourselves? I have no idea how to do that if police are stopping us for the convenience of hit men. What are we supposed to do? Bribe? Bolt? Cower? Plead?

She hits the brakes hard at the edge of the bridge over the Rio Teles Pires. It's an especially rough hundred yards of narrow, cratered concrete. The car behind us is suddenly on our bumper, its lights filling our car and flooding Leonora's face. There's no backing up, no turning off, no dodging, nobody around. Leonora doesn't tell us then, only later, that she feared this was the moment she's been expecting for the last ten years, the moment she finds out for sure what God does with the dead.

On the other hand, maybe they're just following her, keeping tabs on where she goes and who she's with. They do that sometimes.

This nun, it turns out, can drive just fine. The *pistoleiros* stay on us as we rumble over the bridge, then fall back as Leonora picks up what little speed her little car can muster. She veers right onto the highway toward Terra Nova and swerves around a truck piled with furniture and peasants. Just up the road is the little eatery where we'd had lunch that day, run by a family that loves her. I offer the unneeded advice to duck off the highway there. The highway dips for a stretch, then rises, and there's the restaurant. While the car behind us is in the dip, its headlights out of sight, Leonora dives to the left, scoots behind a tree, snaps off the lights. Half a minute later, a car rises from the dip in the road and screams by. It's a dark blue VW Gol.

"That's them," she says.

Promised Land

Glenn Alan Cheney

Chapter Two

Renascer

A lot of people want Sister Leonora Brunetto dead. A lot more — maybe thousands — address her as *Mãe*. Mother. That's not a religious title. Avocationally, she's a Sister. But to fugitive slaves who have hidden in her house, to people who have been camping on the side of roads while waiting for land to which they're constitutionally entitled, to activists who have been guided by her confidence, to women Leonora has coached into their own small businesses, she is addressed as Mãe. As cruel, greedy and ignorant as certain people in Mato Grosso can be, they know what happens if you kill someone's mother.

I asked some men at an *acampamento* — an encampment — called Renascer on a dirt road near Terra Nova what would happen if someone killed Sister Leonora. It was dusk. We sat on crates and logs and busted chairs behind the patchwork hut of a nice, smart man nicknamed Nico. Under stars pinked with the smoke of distant fires, we passed around a *chimarrão*, the bulbous gourd of maté green tea more commonly pictured in the hands of Argentinian gauchos. Everybody sipped from the same steel straw. They rolled thin cigarettes of oily black rope tobacco in rectangles of notebook paper. Little boys growled around the ground, not waiting pushing pictures of trucks and honking at each other.

In his calm, deep, thoughtful voice, Nico said, "Nothing

would happen. The Sister is our hope, and when she's gone, so is our hope. No one will do anything, just as they've never done anything before."

Someone else disagreed, saying that the murder of Leonora would spark people into action. The passivity of the *acampados* would turn violent.

I would have to agree with both of them. The history of the rural poor and landless is one of passive resignation. They suffer the abuse of rich squatters and mercenary polícia militar as if blessed with an infinite capacity to absorb punishment without resisting it. One reason, according to one of Leonora's leaders, is that it's the courageous who get murdered first.

One man at Renascer had been a slave. For 12 years he

worked without pay, slept on the ground, was fed barely enough to say alive. Once he escaped, he did nothing to report the servitude. If he had, he may well have been killed. (In

2009, official s found 22 slavery situations and freed 308 slaves. In all of Brazil in that year, 4,283 slaves were freed. The number of existing slaves is estimated to be several times

that number.)

Nico thinks it would be a good idea for me to interview someone from every household in the camp. He's impressed and grateful that someone from a foreign country has come to witness their most humble life, and he wants everyone in the camp to feel a bit of hope in the international attention. This is what they told me:

As for Nico, his real name is Adoni Medeiros. He's 51. His mother was from Italy, his father part Indian. His first name comes from the Bible, Joshua 10, wherein Adoni was a king of Jerusalem. If Nico has any such title, its Elder of Renascer. For the first part of his life, he worked with the land. Then he spent 15 years driving truck for a timber company and hauling trees out of the forest with a big tractor. Today he doesn't want anything to do with a tractor, except maybe a little one to pull a little plow on a little piece of land. His shack seems to be a little bigger than most in the acampamento. He has a nice enameled wood stove in a porched area behind the house. Fired up, it gushes smoke out the front, but most of it blows away, and whatever blows into the house soon wafts out the walls or seeps through the roof. It isn't the kind of house where smoke would be a problem.

Nico senses that Sister Leonora is getting tired, but he's sure she will not stop until they have their land. He's revolted by people who claim she takes money to prevent progress. "She came from God to be a *guerreira*," he says, a warrior, and without inflection of irony he adds, "If it weren't for that woman, we wouldn't be where we are today."

Antonio, 42, has been here for two and a half years. He says he is courageous but not a hero. Leonora is a hero. She does not give up. She could have her heart cut open, and she would not give up. She would still be where she had to be to talk with someone about what needed to be done. Antonio notes that at Renascer, there are no thieves. You can't say that about many places in Brazil.

Luiz V., 52, was one of the first to arrive at Renascer. Thugs were after him. When he arrived, nine years ago, there was no camp. To sleep, he lay on the ground and wrapped himself in plastic. Today, living alone in the camp, he's torn between staying in the camp, going in to town to care for his parents, who are in their 80s, and looking for work. He goes into town by bike, 87 km, 40 of them dirt. He leaves early in the morning, arrives mid-afternoon.

Luiz used to be afraid of the threats from the *pistoleiros*, thugs, ranchers, and police, but no more. He's in the struggle for all or nothing. And the tension has eased recently.

"Our life here is very hard," he says. "The shacks get rotten and there's no lumber to fix them. The roof leaks. But to give up would be worse than this. Even if I have to eat wood and stone, I will stay here until the end. I'll get my own land some-day, *se Deus quiser*. It's up to Him. We have to wait until He's ready."

His father never had his own land, always worked for other people. He told his son that he never had the right to reap what he sowed, that when you work for others, you never have a future. Luiz's life has been the same so far. He's never had a regular job, just daily work at below minimum wage, no benefits. He has planted trees and then seen them cut down because their owner didn't want them there.

Would he have the strength to start a new farm at his age? He says his energy would double if he had his own land to work. That is his dream: To own his own land. It's a terrible thing, he says, to have a dream and not be able to reach it.

Germira, 67, was camped here until her husband died. Now she lives with her daughter on a lot that was awarded to her in an *asentamento* — a settlement onto land to which she was given title. She keeps a shack in the camp so that maybe someday she can leave a piece of land to her son, an itinerant worker who works for daily pay below minimum wage.

Ivani lives in a pre-*asentamento* just up the road from Renascer. She's been "under the tarp" for seven or eight years. Her house is on a slight hill, and since the floor is the ground, it slants with the hill. It's on land that INCRA — the Instituto Nacional de Colonização e Reforma Agária, the government agency responsible for land redistribution — has awarded her but without the deed and documents that make it really hers. A state judge says he can't give her the deed because it's Union land. But somehow the rancher gets to keep using this Union land. He doesn't respect the boundaries, put up a fence across the land designated to her, but there's nothing she can do about it. "INCRA put us here and abandoned us," she says.

Marlei and her husband, Saul, live a little farther up the road. They, too, have been allocated some land but have yet to receive title to it. INCRA is supposed to send them food and other assistance, but it never arrives. Marlei thinks this is part of a plan to wear them down, let them go broke and force them to move away. Saul says that slavery hasn't ended. It's only been modernized. He is very disappointed in the Partido Trabalhista, the Workers Party led by President Luiz Inácio da Silva, who is known to the world as Lula. The party has so much power, he says: the mayor, a state representative, a senator, the president...why does nothing happen?

Marlei says, "When Leonora sees us suffering, she suffers, too."

Evanete has been living at Renascer for five years. She has four small children. She likes it here, says the people are good and life is quiet. She will wait for her land for as long as it takes.

Nair has been at Renascer for five years after three years at another camp. She's been working the land since she was a child, and her dream is to own her own land. She might start up a chicken or pig business. Her husband picks up field work when he can. They have no children. She says, "God have mercy on us, and when He returns, may He find us on our own land, harvesting things."

Zélia, 63, is thin as can be, lively and talkative. She says she needs medical exams but can't afford them. She had tuberculosis and cancer. She's been five years under the tarp. She is struggling to get land not for herself but for her children and grandchildren. She wishes she had a way to talk to all the poor people to tell them about the struggle.

The people camped at Renascer have been shot, beaten, robbed, arrested, and run out of town. In 2013, a plane sprayed something on the camp and crops planted around it. People got sick, and a planation of banana trees died almost instantly. Around that time someone shot bullets through a house that had children in it. Six people have been murdered. Just up the road, when they tried to occupy some land the federal government had promised them, one man got his spine broken. Several got whipped with fence wire. Skulls got pounded. Bulldozers flattened the camp. A young woman with a baby in her arms screamed at the police as they took her food away. They took everybody's food, the children's school books, everybody's documents, loaded everybody into a truck and dumped them in Terra Nova. It was only with the arrival of federal police that they were allowed to establish the camp where they live now.

But federal police don't just show up. They don't step into land issues without some kind of federal injunction. Federal injunctions don't just happen. Getting them issued takes a lot of brainwork and persistence. Things have to be done right. The process requires an attorney. Somebody needs to make

sure the federal prosecutor receives the papers and that the prosecutor gets the papers to the judge. Somebody might need to remind the judge that he or she got the papers. A state judge might forget. A federal judge might not. Somebody needs to ride herd on all this, and Leonora's about the only one with the time, the sense, and an insistence backed by God. And that's why so many people would prefer to see her dead.

Mato Grosso is not a peaceful place. People kill each other over gold, land, labor, timber, and politics. In 2009, 21 serious threats of death, 13 attempted murders, four murders, and innumerable beatings were reported. Despite the assaults, the people in the camps remain passive,

fearing that the least mis-
demeanor will eradicate the
little progress they've made
in courts. They also fear the
polícia militar, against whom
they have no defense.

Still, a few quietly — always quietly — suggest that
violence might provide the
oomph that gets INCRA to
take action. Oddly enough, I
never heard that from anyone
in a camp, only from sympa-
thetic people in town.

But the people in the
camps deeply resent having
to live in shacks on a narrow
strip of land across the road
from prima dona cattle in an
endless Eden of grass.

"We have nothing, and
they have everything," Nico
tells me. They being the cattle, fat hump-backed brahmas within 50 feet of his
hut. They have six thousand
hectares; the camp has two.

(A hectare is about 2.5 acres.) They have all the food they can eat; the camp lives on minimal nutrition sent occasionally by INCRA. They are protected by the police; the camp is assaulted by the police. They get medical care; people don't. They have electricity; the camp is in the dark.

And they are vulnerable. The six thousand cattle on that farm across the road are overseen by no more than half a dozen farmhands. A handful of peasants could do a lot of damage. They could make the ranch unviable. No one at this camp suggested such action, but it must have occurred to them. But there would be two problems: One would be the bulldozers, fires, broken backs, whippings, and gunfire. The other is a five-foot-two sister called Mother. She says *No*. And that may be one reason why no one has killed her.

Promised Land

Chapter Three

Agrarian Reform

In 1988, the principle of agrarian land redistribution was written into the country's new constitution. It allows the government to appropriate unproductive rural land, with compensation to the owner, for redistribution to small farmers. It also calls for the distribution of land that has always belonged to "the Union," even if occupied. INCRA oversees the agrarian reform.

The common misconception is that the land to be redistributed is owned by the ranchers and farmers who have fenced it in. In fact, unless the land has been specifically sold to them, it still belongs to the Union. Though they may be millionaires claiming tens of thousand of hectares, they are, in fact, squatters. By hook or crook some have managed to get the land registered as their own. Fake deeds float around Mato Grosso like so many buzzards riding the heat waves that ripple off the grass where the forest used to be. Vast tracts of soy fields and pasture have been bought, sold, subdivided, even inherited. Those who cleared the rainforest or think they bought a legitimate piece of property will not give it up easily. Some kill to keep it. Some will even kill a nun.

INCRA moves very slowly. (Leonora notes that if you add a *"do"* to the end of INCRA, you get a participle that means "clogged.") It lacks personnel and political will. It works within a horrendous bureaucracy. The deeds and documents it deals with are complex and often compromised. Judges and politicians, often big-time squatters themselves, have little impetus to make the law work. Land transfers that could be done in 60 days haven't been effected in a decade.

Leonora and I went to the INCRA office in Colíder to nudge a transfer that's been in the works for years. The manager there seems sincere in his desire to get the issue wrapped up and done with, but he reminds her of all the obstacles that are beyond his control.

Afterward, on the sidewalk outside the office, we talk with one her leaders, Valdir, who lives in an acampamento outside of Nova Canãa. His cell phone rings. The caller, his ID blocked, calls him a shameless dog and informs him that this is the day he will die. He adds a crude comment about Leonora.

In the car, on the way back to Terra Nova, me at the wheel,

nervous, eye in the rear-view, Leonora tells me that "they" tap her phone and the phones of everyone she calls. "They" are the ranchers, the polícia militar, and, she suspects, Brazil's federal intelligence agency. Once they got the tapping technology wrong and she could hear them in the background. She thinks it was the police because she could hear them beating somebody. Sometimes a car full of thugs will follow her. Outside of the INCRA office they knew she was talking with Valdir. They know where she's going now, and they know who's in the car with her. They make these death threats, she says, because they know they're losing.

* * *

Here's the deal with the landless camps. Somebody does some research at a local house of bureaucracy, called a forum, and identifies a piece of land that has always belonged to the Union. If it's Union land, citizens are entitled to a piece of it. A bunch of them get organized, usually under one of two organizations: the Movimento dos Sem Terras (MST, the Movement of the Landless) or the Comissão Pastoral da Terra (CPT, the Pastoral Land Commission). In a surprise swoop they set up camp on or adjacent to the land they claim. Since land along highways is Union land, that's where the camps tend to appear — a few dozen or a couple hundred people on a gravely swath between the asphalt and a barbed wire fence.

And there they stay in ramshackle hovels that alternately

swelter and leak. They pull their water from wells, bathe from buckets, cook over wood fires in clay ovens. They do their squatting over holes within walls of plastic sheets. They light their hovels with home-made kerosene lamps, just twists of cotton stuck in cans, the little flames sending up oily black wiggles of smoke. Men go off to look for field work. Women keep clothes and homes remarkably clean, their pots and pans aston-ishingly shiny. A school bus  picks up the children every morning and brings them home a little wiser. Some people give up. Some stick it out. Some have been there for eight years or more.

Each acampamento elects leaders and makes decisions much in the way of New England town meetings. Drug use, prostitution, and drunkenness are strictly prohibited. The camp can vote to expel abusers.

Sometimes an acampamento turns into an invasão, a rush into a pasture that soon becomes an ocupação. When the po-lice or thugs arrive, it turns into a *despejo*, an ejection, and then it's back to the acampamento with everyone who sur-vives or doesn't flee. Every once in a while a judge grants some campers or occupiers permission to remain on the plots they have claimed, though it may take INCRA many years to untangle and reassemble the paperwork needed for the issuance of deeds. That's a *pre-asentamento,* a pre-settlement. How long that claim holds up without deeds, or how long until the deeds actually get issued, depends on how much time attorneys are willing to contribute to the effort, whether judges die, retire, move on, or get bought off, and how much pressure the CPT or MST puts on INCRA and the courts. On rare occasions, an actual *asentamento* happens, and the people entitled to the land actually get the titles that verify ownership.

The Comissão Pastoral da Terra was formed in 1975. The military government that had taken over in 1964 was pushing hard to grow the national economy even when the migration of wealth to the upper class meant deeper impoverishment of the lower classes, especially rural peasants. Small farmers were forced off their land by dam projects, drought, mines, and ranchers willing to use brute force to take what they wanted. The CPT was formed by the National Conference of the Bishops of Brazil. The Lutheran Church of Brazil later backed the organization. CPT activities began in the Amazon region but soon spread throughout Brazil, struggling to protect small farms, combat slavery and protect escaped slaves, protect the environment, defend water supplies, and generally help the poor, women, migrants, Indians, and anyone else being overrun by capitalism, dictatorship, and modernity.

The Movimento dos Sem-Terras was formed in 1983 in the south of Brazil in defense of people whose land was in one

way or another tak-
en and swallowed
by bigger farms.
The organization
is more tightly fo-
cused on agrarian
reform than CPT is,
and it is more vo-
ciferous and rigid,
arguably to a fault.

Leonora compares its structure and discipline to that of an army. The MST is more likely to suffer violence after occupying land, blocking roads, or pressuring INCRA and others through obstructive rowdiness. MST pushes harder, demanding action and threatening civil disobedience if not outright violence. The organization charges a substantial fee — effectively rent — from people in its camps. CPT collects R$ 3 per family year just to support a fund for the occasional ambulance ride or other emergency.

CPT uses a more passive, almost Gandhian strategy, demanding rights and land but waiting patiently, peacefully, almost as if offering people's suffering as an obvious reason to take land from the few and divide it among the many.

The CPT became especially active in Mato Grosso, which was becoming the front line between raw nature and crude capitalism. The greedy were exploiting nature for all it offered: first wood, then gold, then what little soil remained atop the gravel that underlies most of the Amazonian biome. This economy, based on theft from nature, isn't worthy of being called capitalism. It involves very little capital. The capital invested in a ranch amounts to little more than fencing. Since productive land is in so few hands, few people benefit from it.

It takes about one hectare of grass to feed one head of cattle. A pasture of ten thousand hectares yields a lot of beef. But the beef gets exported and the cash goes to a wealthy absentee squatter. The whole business employs only a handful of people. During the dry months — June and July — many ranchers burn their fields to put a bit of nutrients back into the soil. The nutrients go up in smoke, too, and pretty soon not even grass will grow. As vegetation disappears, the streams and springs dry up. The final stage of this primitive capitalism will be a wasteland.

This scenario isn't of a future generation. It's already happening. Eco-agronomist Epifânia Rita Vuaden gives the region another five or ten years. "The dime has dropped," she says. "It's already happening. Terra Nova has already lost 56 springs. Some areas cannot be farmed anymore. People have just abandoned their land. It's dead."

She knows 20-year-olds who have never seen a forest. When their parents were that age, there was nothing here but forest.

She says this with a hand on her belly. She's pregnant.

In cahoots with Sister Leonora and a number of sponsors and social organizations, Epifânia is cranking up a project to begin reforesting the area. Under the law at that time, land-owners must keep 80 percent of their property in natural, native forest. Forest must be left intact within 30 meters of streams and springs. But the law means little in Mato Grosso, so virtually no one has preserved the required forest. And really, it's unrealistic to expect them to do so. If the farmers of the American midwest left 80 percent of their land to its natural ecosystem, the United States wouldn't have much of a breadbasket.

But Epifânia says that a hectare of natural forest produc-

es more economic benefit — nuts, fruits, wood, materials — than the single cattle that needs a hectare of grass. The economic difference is that a few people can oversee thousands of hectares of pasture, but harvesting a forest is more labor intensive. A rich guy in São Paulo can't do it or have it done. It's the work of a family. The fifty

Epifânia Vuaden

thousand hectares of pasture that benefits a single owner and feeds no one in Brazil could benefit 500 families on plots of a hundred hectares, a size that would allow 80 percent as forest with the rest dedicated to garden, a small field for cash crops, and a couple of dairy cows.

The Instituto Brasileira de Geografia e Estatística, a government agency, says that in 2006, 2.8 percent of rural properties were large farms. They occupied 56.7 percent of the country's arable land. Small properties represented 62.2 percent of rural properties but occupied only 7.9 percent of arable land.

Epifânia's Seed Project pays people to bring native tree seeds to a depository in Terra Nova. Many of the seed gatherers are peasants who know the forest, have time to seek out seeds, and can use the cash. The project the mixes up a muvuca, a carefully formulated hodgepodge of seeds. Some will sprout early, grow fast, and provide something that can be harvested — corn, for example. That early growth provides shade for a fast-growing tree — balsa, for example — that can be harvested in a few years. In its shade will sprout trees of longer term. Come rainy season — it used to start in August, now September, in 2010 only in October — a muvuca gets planted in a one-meter square patch dug a few inches deep, with patches spaced by a few meters. The nascent rainforest will need to be thinned every once in a while. Other than that, it's on automatic. The plan is to plant 200 metric tons of seed on 1,200 hectares.

CPT's mission is far more comprehensive than MST's. It is decentralized enough to take shape and assume goals as appropriate in any given region. In Mato Grosso it formed an association in 1979 to help people who had been thrown off their land. One such case was that of Enrico Trindade. He and 130 families lived on small farms in an area next to land that someone from Portugal had bought. The Portuguese wanted to buy their land, but they refused to sell. The effort to dislodge them turned violent, and in 1982 Trindade, who headed an association of the families, was killed, and his son was gravely wounded. The violence was instigated by the polícia militar and *pistoleiros* hired by the rancher. The CPT joined with other social movements to demand justice. The government called for testimony, but no one showed up. At a second hearing, witnesses showed up, but the judge didn't. Similar problems continued for 24 years. The case never came to trial. The associated movements referred the case to the Organization of American States, which has the power to condemn a country that does not practice what its laws preach. The OAS condemned Brazil, and its government was suitably embarrassed. But embarrassment is about all that came of the killings and the dysfunctional legal system, and embarrassment is something Brazil has learned to deal with.

In northern Mato Grosso, the face of the CPT is that of Sister Leonora: brown-eyed, softly wrinkled, quick to smile, and always, under any pressure or bearing the worst of news, warm and motherly. She has been a sister or training to be one since 1959, when, as a teenager, she left home in the south of Brazil to join the Irmãs de Encantado congregation. They put

her through high school   on a track to become a teacher. She
soon went to work in the poorest areas of the city, where she
could not accept people's misery, hunger, and abandonment.
she took her voews with the Irmãs do Imaculado Coração da
Maria — the Sisters of the Immaculate Heart of Maria — and
has been "in the struggle" ever since.

She does not struggle alone. Her congregation, though
literally a thousand miles away, backs her with prayer and
occasional respite. A handful of sisters offer support in Mato
Grosso: Sr. Nilza Sulzback, Sr. Rosamélia Gonzatti, Sr. Ilga
Fell, and Sr. Lara Pissatto. Several activists, some of whom
prefer to remain anonymous, keep Leonora's projects alive
— Dorvalino, Nevair and his wife, Valdir and his wife, Lin-
domar, Joseja, Ivani, Bete, Darci, Norma, Everaldo, Joãozin-
ho, Silvio and his wife, Cleusa, Márcio, Niom, Alain and his

family, Alderi, Elizete, Mariza and her husband, Hézio, Teobaldo, Negão, Nelso, and many others, several of whom are mentioned elsewhere in this book.

It's a small group, however, and it faces a large and powerful opposition that includes elected officials in Brasilia, wealthy landowners in São Paulo, corrupt judges in Mato Grosso, and not a few citizens who confuse Christian activism with Communist plots.

But Leonora does what she must do and goes where she must go to comfort people who call her Mãe. Her presence gives them hope. The default expression on her motherly face: *The situation is serious but it's going to be all right.* Her default message: *Don't give up.*

Glenn Alan Cheney

Chapter Four

The Law Here Is Money

To keep the several hundred people at the acampamento Cinco Estrelas from giving up, she manages to get the Brazilian Commission on Human Rights to send a team to the camp. They shove off from the Hotel Avenida in Terra Nova shortly after dawn, one federal "Highway Police" at the wheel of each of four cars. I don't know what Brazil feeds its Highway Police, but these seem a lot bigger than the state polícia militar and everyone else in town. Dressed in camouflage fatigues and dark glasses, each carries a 9mm automatic, a bowie knife strapped to the thigh, enough ammunition to hold out for a while, handcuffs and other gadgets of the law. They wear thick, black bulletproof vests and crush hats snapped up on the sides. In one car they have at least one machine gun, just in case. They look grim, alert, suspicious, worried. They do the driving. Leonora rides in the back seat. I get to ride in front with agent Marco Antônio, who doesn't seem to like me. I have a feeling I'm a complication.

Cinco Estrelas is outside of Novo Mundo, a town 32 kilometers off Brazil Route 163. Some 180 families live in little homes of hardwood frames and veneer-thin slats of a soft wood. The roofs are plastic sheets with palm leaves tossed over them for a bit of shade and to keep the plastic from flapping. The floors are dirt, of course. The camp is clean, free of litter and garbage. They haul the water eight meters out of wells and dump it into plastic barrels with a spout at the bottom. Their outhouses have no roofs, but the walls are thick planks of rare tropical hardwood.

The land they've been promised is just across the road, the Fazenda Cinco Estrelas. The current squatter, Osmar Rodrigues-Cunha, bought it from Sebastião Neves, a.k.a. Chapeu Preto — Black Hat — a renowned pistoleiro who owns a few farms and administers a few others, hundreds of thousands of acres in all. His men have chased Sister Leonora for as long as three days. He has accused her of sending hit squads after him. He's been arrested for such things as slavery and illegal land deals, but he never spent more than token time behind bars.

The Human Rights team includes an attorney, a psychologist, a sociologist, a security technician, and a guy in charge.

They are visiting Cinco Estrelas to learn the extent to which the people here have been forgotten by the law and the psychological impact of living under daily threats of death. They will conclude something and write a report. The Highway Police hang out in the shade of a hut while a couple dozen residents gather in a circle under a roofed area be-  hind a little house. Sister Leonora explains why the visitors have come all the way from Brasilia.

In simple, graphic, ungrammatical terms, the residents report the stress they've been under. At first they take turns, but the testimonies soon break down into extrapolations of each other's stories.

Seven people have been murdered. One young man was granted permission to fish on private property, then shot for trespassing. Another got axed in the head and took six months to die. Another disappeared. Almost every day they receive death threats hollered out the window of a car or phoned into someone's cell phone. When they go into Novo Mundo, tough guys hound them. Their motorbikes get run off the road. Their children are threatened at the bus stop. When the men look for field work, no one will hire them. At night, motorcyclists shout threats from the road. Their tarps have bullet holes. With most of the men off looking for work, it wouldn't take many armed men to invade the camp and have their way with it.

On February 21, 2010, four months before the commission arrived, 22 military police and associated thugs ran ev-

erybody off the land, burned the camp, bulldozed everything. The people fled to Guarantã do Norte and stormed the INCRA office. They stayed for 35 days, demanding the land they'd been promised for so long. Finally, some federal support came along, and everyone got to go back and build another camp.

The people are angry because there's no reason for the delay in granting land titles. The federal government is sure it owns the land that Fazenda Cinco Estrelas illegally occupies. INCRA expresses every intention of deeding the land to the campers. Family plots have already been laid out. So why doesn't it happen?

"We want an answer," says one man, palms tilted to the sky.

Another offers an answer, "The law here is money. Who has the money determines the law."

An old man says "Seven years under the tarp is a long time."

A younger man says, "What do they want us to do? Go to a slum somewhere and live by robbing people? Do they want us to mine for gold? Do they want us to raise pirate cattle and not pay taxes on them?"

Another says, "We have no security here. They could come any night and kill us all."

Another has a joke: "We aren't landless. We have land. It's under our fingernails." During the meeting, somebody spots smoke rising from behind a hill a kilometer and a half away. It quickly turns blacker, seemingly angrier and closer. This has happened before. Someone sets a fire near the camp, hoping that either the camp burns or the people in it get blamed for the fire. Leonora notes that at least this time they have federal witnesses. Two guys start up a motorcycle to go investigate. Leonora tells them to be careful, not to risk too much.

In apologetic tones, the commission attorney admits that his group doesn't own the government and can't resolve the agrarian reform issues. "Our main concern here," he says, "is to keep you alive and continuing the struggle."

Leonora tells me later that the only purpose of the meeting was to show some federal presence and give people enough hope to hang on a little longer. The federal presence also makes her a little more secure. She's less likely to be gunned down if the bad guys think the repercussions might reach Brasília.

Promised Land

Glenn Alan Cheney

Chapter Five

Leonora Hunted

L eonora needs a well armed federal escort for good reason.
In 2005, a few years after she had arrived in the area, she
was helping a community organization establish a little facto-
ry to process Brazil nuts. It's a good product for the region because the nuts come from the stately castanheira tree, which
can grow to a height of 35 to 40 meters. You can still see
some of their charred skeletons in the pastures along BR-163,
eerily majestic with their tall, straight trunks, unbranched on
their lower half. It takes a long, long time to grow a castanheira from scratch, and the trees planted in plantations produce few nuts. The tree needs specialized bees to pollinate its
deep blossoms, and these bees live only in the forest. As pro-

ducers of nuts, they serve as economic justification for leaving the forest alive. All to0 often, however, a rancher-squatter will prefer the immediate value of the castanheira wood over the long-term value of annual harvests of nuts. Since his ranch will probably dry up and blow away in a few years, the financially smart decision is to take the wood.

But enough castanheiras remained in 2005 for a community to turn them into a business. Leonora was there to help them get organized. She didn't know that the mayor of the town had somehow turned the coordinator of the project against her. When he failed to appear at a certain meeting, Leonora asked his wife where he'd gone. The wife said he'd felt sick and gone to the hospital. That didn't make sense to Leonora. She already had a sixth sense of suspicion and recognized the situation as "black, ugly." The coordinator had actually gone to fetch the *pistoleiros* who were supposed to come eliminate her. When his wife invited Leonora to spend the night at their house, she resisted but eventually agreed. But once there, the wife insisted that she sleep with her window open. Leonora then knew something was up. After much insistence and counter-insistence, Leonora shut the window, and the wife went to bed. Leonora went to talk with the young man who was driving her around, told him to be alert, something was wrong.

She stayed awake all that night, pacing around her room to stay awake. Once the woman came back to peek in to see if she was sleeping, which Leonora pretended to be doing. At five o'clock she came out of her room and declined to have breakfast in the house. She told the woman that she had to

go to a certain other community. But that was only a ruse to throw off whoever might be coming to get her. Still unsure what was happening — only later would she learn that the

coordinator hadn't found the *pistoleiros* because they were off killing somebody else — she went back to the community center. She was giving a training session when the *pistoleiros* showed up outside. She recognized one of them from the assault on the Renascer acampamento.

She thought the best thing to do was to keep on with the training. The killers wouldn't do their business among of bunch of people. She called her driver and told him to be ready. They would have to get away somehow.

At about 11:30 she announced lunch and told everyone that they could rest afterward but if anyone wanted to accompany her to the other community, she'd be going there and returning that afternoon. Again, it was a ruse. During lunch, she stayed with the children, sacrosanct territory even for hired killers. She called Father Vitório. He said he'd send a car to meet her on the other side of the Rio Teles Pires, at the ferry

landing. At a moment of opportunity, she slipped out one door
and the driver slipped out the other. The driver took off in the
car, hoping to draw the killer away. But they stayed, apparently figuring on killing her after she returned.

There was a truck nearby. Leonora pleaded with the driver to take her to the ferry at the river, but she made the mis-
take of telling him why. He refused to risk his life. Leonora
said that if they took a few children, they'd be safe until she
got out at the ferry. So he took her.

Then the ferry operator refused to take her across the river until a car arrived. He wasn't going to do it for just one
person She begged him, offered any price, but he said they
only had a wait a few minutes. He could see the dust from a
car that was arriving.

It was the dust of the *pistoleiros*. Leonora asked if she
could ride in the little tugboat that pushed the ferry across the
river. The operator let her. She hid there while her hunters
and their car rode the ferry.

Waiting on the other side was Ivaine, a church activist.
As soon as the ferry landed, Leonora jumped ashore and disappeared into a group of people. It so happened that Ivaine's
driver was a friend of the guy driving for the *pistoleiros*. He
went over to talk with his friend, who then became afraid
because he'd been recognized. He and the killer drove off
toward Carlinda, some 60 km away. Ivaine took Leonora to
the house of someone in his driver's family. They forgot to
lock the car when they got out. Within minutes, the *pistoleiros*

Glenn Alan Cheney

found the the car and stole the driver's documents from it. Ivaine sent someone to scout around for the killers and found them waiting at a fork in the road out of town. He and Leonora took a different road and drove to his house, where his wife, Bete, four months pregnant, had just received a phone call telling her that Ivaine was with Leonora and would not be coming home ever again.

They arrived safely and spent the night. The next morning there was a meeting at the house — some church people, a banker, and someone from the government — to finalize a credit agreement. The pistoleiro's car passed by outside. Ivaine's phone rang. It was them, telling the people to send Leonora out or they would come in and kill everybody. Ivaine suggested they come in to do their killing so a few of them could get killed, too.

They called Padre Vitório. He said he would swing by in his truck. They timed it so that he passed the house just as the *pistoleiros* were going around the block. Vitório took her to his house. She spent the night there, but by morning, the *pistoleiros* found her. Vitório managed to get ahold of an honest state representative. The rep got ahold of the polícia federal, and a few hours later they arrived in three cars. They took Leonora and the rep to Cuiabá, and from there Leonora went to Brasilia, where law and order are more respected, though it wasn't too long before Brazil's Minister of Justice asked her to leave town before something ugly happened.

During the days of this 2005 episode, Sister Dorothy

39

Stang, an American from Dayton, Ohio, working in the state of Pará, to the northeast of Mato Grosso, was shot dead while walking down a road alone. She was 73. She'd been doing work much like Leonora's, defending the forest and promoting sustainable use of it. The man accused of ordering her murder, Vitalmiro Bastos de Moura, was convicted after his trigger-man, Rayfran das Neves Sales, implicated him. But in a second trial — mandatory for sentences of over 20 years — Sales said he'd acted alone. After an international uproar, a panel of judges later overturned the exoneration, and a subsequent trial returned Moura to a 30-year sentence, though he was subsequently released pending an appeal. In 2013 the appeal failed, and the sentence was confirmed. Neves Sales was given a 27-year sentence, but he was released after serving less than a third of that. Another defendant, Regivaldo Galvão, was convicted in May of 2010 but was granted conditional release in 2012.

* * *

José Evenaldo de Souza Mecedo, an attorney, used to help Leonora with legal issues, but he had to distance himself from her. He had lived in Terra Nova for about ten years. Having been educated in a seminary, he has always been willing to help Leonora in her many ongoing legal efforts. On three occasions, he and his brother whisked her out of town when thugs came after her. He got a bad reputation among big ranchers. One day the police killed somebody and then arrested Mecedo for the murder. He had eye witnesses who could prove his innocence, but that wasn't enough. He contacted the federal Commission on Human Rights and affirmed that the police had killed the victim and that a group of ranchers were behind the murder. But there was no investigation. Under threats from the police in Terra Nova, he moved to Sinop, where, he says, "The police are a little less personal." His case is still open.

"That's is how they get rid of leaders," he says. "You can't help Leonora openly. It has to be done in secret."

One reason Sister Leonora hasn't been killed, Mecedo says, is the international attention given to the murder of Dorothy Stang and the conviction, however temporary, of five conspirators. The news of the murders and court cases was reported around the world. The international attention helped focus federal attention, and the killing of a second elderly Sister would likely accomplish the same. Not that murderers are always caught, but these days it's a possibility.

In 2006, Leonora had some people from an acampamento staying with her for a few days. The visitors went out for a while. Leonora was in the apartment attached to her house, just across a tiled breezeway from her front door. She heard a noise and peeked out. Voices. She softly closed the door, locked it, and turned off the light in the bathroom. Someone said, "She's not here, let's just get the materials." They went into her office, took everything that contained information:

documents, CDs, tapes, and a DVD with a video of police beating people who had tried to occupy land on a ranch. Among the papers was a report about all the people who had been murdered in the region in recent years. After they left, Leonora ran to a neighbor and stayed there until her visitors

In 2007, a neighbor noticed a blue Chevette driving past Leonora's house several times. At around 7:00 p.m. the neighbor saw men coming into the yard. She called Leonora and told her to quickly lock herself in the house. Leonora was alone, but some other sisters and a visitor from an acampamento were in the street somewhere. Leonora called a lawyer who had a home and office nearby and asked her to find the sisters and warn them. The sister returned to report a rumor that men were coming to eliminate Leonora. Later that night, the men returned and tried to get the door open. The visitor from the camp guarded Leonora's car all night. When he returned to the camp the next day, someone shot him, though not fatally. Leonora called the Federal Police. They could not come to help her, so they told her to go to Sinop, a town two hours away. Another lawyer-friend came and got her car and hid it somewhere. Later, after dark, someone picked her up and drove her to her car. The lawyer drove her to Sinop. Only after they arrived did he tell her that he'd been trying to stay ahead of a car that was following them. From Sinop Leonora went to Brasilia and stayed for three months.

*　　*　　*

Leonora feels a little safer if I'm around. Half a mile from downtown, at Terra Nova's only restaurant beside a pond that provides its fish, she tells me she wouldn't be this far from downtown if I weren't there. Not that she thinks I'm bullet-proof, but a murdered foreigner would draw international attention. When she invites me to stay in an apartment attached to her house, I resist until I realize she wants somebody there,

a potential witness. So I move out of the Hotel Avenida, and there I am, rooming with a nun. We have meals togeth-er along with her housemate, Sister Nilsa, a sweet, humble, muttering woman who teaches homeopathy and stays out of politics. I do some of the cooking. I wash dishes. We talk a lot. I hear horror stories of priests, nuns, and peasants mur-

dered, widespread slavery, the organized crime family of police, ranchers, and politicians. I am to trust no one and I am
not to tell anywhere where she goes, I go, or either one of us
went or will go.

A week after I move in, however, the situation at Cinco
Estrelas heats up. A judge in Cuiabá is about to sign a paper
that will go to the Supreme Court in Brasilia. Leonora will
have to go there — a bus trip of over 32 hours — to represent
her people. If she's not there, the process of the last eight
years returns to the state courts, a setback of years. The re-
sults at the Supreme Court will be a roll of dice — some of the
judges respect law; some are self-interested. Just one of them
will make the decision. She doesn't know who it will be.

Two guys from the acampamento come to the house. Leonora gives them firm instructions: Be prepared to move fast.
As soon the Supreme Court judge signs the paper, the acampamento has to move onto the farm. If the rancher-squatter,
who's associated with the killer/slave owner Chapeu Preto,
isn't there and the new residents are, it's unlikely they'll be
told to leave. Everyone knows where their plot of land is. They
are to quickly set up houses and start planting. They are to
stay out of the reserved forest area. "If anyone goes in there,
friend or foe, call the police," she says. "If somebody goes
in there and cuts wood or starts a fire, they're going to blame
it on us." Be alert. Form groups and stick together. Hold a
meeting; make sure everybody knows what they're supposed
to do. "For the love of God," she says, "do not touch any farm

equipment that's still there. Settle near the main house but do not go inside. Make sure everyone knows what to do and what not to do. No mistakes or we lose everything."

At this first stage, no one will own a particular piece of land. They'll simply be assigned a place where they can live and plant. For the time being, the whole piece of land will be an agrovila, a village owned by everybody. They need to quickly establish where their school, church, clinic and public spaces will be. "This is just like farming," Leonora tells the men from the camp. "You have to plan things or you'll just kill yourself with work."

That night she gets a call from the local police. She has to clear out of town by morning because someone's coming to kill her to keep her from getting to Brasilia. Sister Nilsa has to disappear, too. And she'd better get that foreigner out of her house because how does she know who he really is. So it's back to the Hotel Avenida with me, and for the next week no one knows where Leonora is. Then she shows up. The judge in Cuiabá didn't sign the paper. There's no danger yet, but Cinco Estrelas, she tells me, is on war footing.

Promised Land

Glenn Alan Cheney

Chapter Six

Pioneers

A few years ago, Elizete stopped going places in Leonora's car. It was too dangerous. At the time, they were driving around the outback areas of Terra Nova gathering data for a municipal plan of sustainable development. Some of the big landowners were getting desperate to stop the agrarian reform. Leonora represented too much hope. The lonely dirt roads offered easy places for an ambush. Even as an employee of town hall, Elizete wouldn't necessarily be spared. She had children to support and a grandson on the way. Riding around with a sister with a price on her head was irresponsible.

Elizete belongs to the most revered class of people in Terra Nova — the pioneiros. She arrived there in 1978 on one of the first four buses of pioneers. She was five years old. The settlers were being relocated after getting chased off an Indian reservation in Rio Grande do Sul, Brazil's southernmost state. They were camped on the grounds of an agricultural fair. The fair was to open soon, so the government pulled together a settlement plan in the state of Mato Grosso — Dense Forest — and off they went. It was below freezing when they got on the bus and sweltering when they got off many days later in the middle of a jungle. To a little girl who had heard tales of jaguars and anacondas, the trees were dark and ominous in the dusk. A truck took the little family to their assigned lot deep in the forest. Elizete remembers the panic in her father's face, the tears bubbling in her mother's eyes. There was supposed to be a pre-fabricated house waiting for them, but all they found was a black tarp over two sticks. They had no food whatsoever. When the truck came back with another family, Paulo, pushing off the protests of his panic-stricken wife, Gersi, grabbed a ride back to the main road, where he managed to get some water, powdered milk, and a little food. Then he walked back. Working in the dark, they spread a sheet on the ground under the tarp, and the five of them cowered together in a cacophony of animal sounds.

The settlement was part of a government plan to repopulate the Amazon region. (The previous population of northern Mato Grosso — the Manitsauá, Kren Akarore, Apiraká, Kayabí, and other tribes, had been massacred or moved to the Xingu reservation, freeing the forest for the military to use as a wilderness training ground.) A Lutheran minister from Rio Grande do Sul, Norberto Schwantes, was orchestrating the project under a co-op called Coopercana. Coopercana was to manage government assistance, provide housing and agricultural support services, receive and distribute government food packages, operate schools and clinics, build roads, buy and market whatever the settlers managed to grow, and otherwise oversee the blossoming of civilization in the jungle.

Like just about everything in Brazil, however, the plan got bollixed up and corrupted. The permanent housing never arrived. Neither did the mule and cart they'd been promised. The government sent food, sometimes by helicopter, but somehow some of it ended up for sale in Alta Floresta, 200 kilometers to the north. Elizete's father, Paulo Pinheiro, remembers having to spend all day on buses to go buy powdered milk — his powdered milk — that the co-op had sold to a store. The settlers were at Coopercana's mercy. They had no way of knowing what aid was coming from the government and no way to communicate with the outside world. Coopercana was a Big Brother and not an especially benevolent one.

Life was very difficult. Malaria was common. Income was minimal. The co-op never paid much for crops. Law was distant. Many people gave up and returned to the south. Elizete remembers a day when a bus drove by and something shiny and colorful came fluttering out a window. She and her little friends ran to get it. It was cellophane from a package of cookies. Its texture and colors seemed magical, and it smelled otherworldly. She and her little brother licked it for everything they could get. Paulo's brother came to settle in the area and brought his eight kids. When he died of malaria, the kids moved in with Paulo and family — 11 children in house barely big enough for three. The stress of tight quarters, little food, and no security pushed the family toward hostility and insanity. The bickering, fighting, and familial chaos were almost constant. Paulo got involved with bad men, *pistoleiros*. Once Elizete heard him and some others plotting to go kill someone while the family was at church, but she doesn't know if they actually did it. One stormy night somebody shot bullets through their house. Paulo, unable to accept the whole situation, had nervous breakdowns and attempted suicide at least four times.

Paulo remembers being told that if he didn't clear his 200 hectares, especially the trees around the springs and rivers, he could lose his land. He did as told. Nature was the enemy. The forest sheltered jaguars that could devour a child. He knew of two men who had been devoured by snakes. A snake ate the family dog, a forty-pound mutt named Tigre. The forest was the enemy camp; the pasture was civilization. The more pasture he had around his house, the safer and better fed his family.

Elizete loved to read. She read everything with words on it, from romance novels to information that came with medications. But her father saw no point in a girl reading or getting educated beyond the basics. Education was for boys. Her role in life was to be a good wife. She had thoughts, however, of becoming a doctor and a missionary nun. She corresponded with Camillian nuns. Her father hated the idea as much as he hated nuns, priests, and church.

Elizete was on a volleyball team when she attracted the eye of a young man, a handsome blonde of Italian descent who, like most of the families, had come from the south of Brazil. All the girls had crushes on him, but his crush was on Elizete. They became friends, and pretty soon they were doing a lot of kissing and such. Before long, her father found out and prohibited the relationship. She was only 13. The boy was 21. Her father's opinion mattered nothing to her. He had never offered her affection, and home was a hell of mayhem and conflict. She was 14 when she ran off with the boy and married him. They lived in a shed behind is family's house on a relatively large and prosperous rice farm. She barely understood how a girl gets pregnant and had no idea how it might be prevented. She only knew that sex hurt. She tried to avoid it, but she didn't avoid it enough. Less than a month after her fifteenth birthday, she went into labor. The family refused to take her to the hospital. A midwife handled the delivery. After a night of unspeakable agony, Elizete delivered an eight-pound boy.

Meanwhile, her little brother, a shy and quiet boy who had always been afraid to speak, ran away from home. He wanted to become a priest so that he would never have to get married or have children. Elizete thought maybe he could go be educated by the Camillian sisters. They agreed, but he had to get his father's permission because he was only 13. After much pressure, his father agreed, but only under the condition that the boy not become a priest. The boy left and did not return until he was 26, a teacher with a Master's degree.

Elizete loved her little boy and found all joy in him. Her in-laws, snobbish in their perceived superiority to Brazilians unendowed with Italian genes, made her feel like the lowest of human creatures. Most of the time her husband ignored her. She found respect when, at the age of 18, she was elected president of her community association. They held dances and festivals, formed a theater group, collected food for the poor. Everybody wanted her to be their children's godmother. But when she attempted to defend the poor by telling a priest that they shouldn't have to pay a tithe, she fell under criticism of the church and rich land owners. She resigned from her position, dropped out of the community, just stayed home in a state of sadness and anger. She began to suffer unidentifiable maladies. Her weight dropped to 88 pounds.

Barely 20, she started to wonder if whether children and housekeeping were all she could get from life. She kept reading and reading and reading. She read a religious family magazine and enjoyed the column called "Filosofia" even though she didn't know what the word meant. She just knew that it made her feel somehow oriented, made her question herself and motivated her to seek something. It offered proverbs and quotes, St. Francis of Assis saying, "Begin by doing the necessary, then do what's possible, and soon you will be doing the impossible," and somebody else saying, "Believe in time, in friendship, in wisdom, and mainly in love; take time for dreams...they will take your carriage to the stars."

Someone gave her a big, thick book titled *Pérolas da Vida* — Pearls of life. She read it all. At the bus station one day, waiting to take her son to the doctor for a vaccination, she met a man selling books. Her husband had told her not to spend any money because he needed it to go to a soccer game that weekend. But the books looked so delicious, so tempting, especially one on yoga, something she'd barely heard of. She talked the man into a big discount and almost got beat up when she returned home.

She borrowed romance novels from someone who had a collection, and she imagined falling in love with an imaginary man who really loved her, respected her dreams, believed she could accomplish something and wanted her to study and learn. She wrote six volumes of diary and kept them well hidden. No one ever saw them or knew how she felt. Then one day she got depressed and burned them all.

And then she found herself pregnant again. When the big day came, she went to the hospital alone and gave birth to a girl. Although she kept her dreams, she put them aside while she raised her son and daughter. As long as they were happy and growing, she was happy enough. But she felt herself an extraterrestrial on a strange planet. She found no joy in meeting with other women to gossip and sip a chimarrão. And she didn't want to get fat like those women, so she stayed home and practiced yoga from the book.

She kept getting sick without apparent cause. Though she felt she was killing herself with medication, she took birth control pills. Nonetheless, at the age of 21 she found herself pregnant once again. She thought about abortion but also thought about how nice it was to have a baby. It was a difficult pregnancy. She was always on the verge of miscarriage. A few weeks before her due date, the doctor sensed a problem, put her in his car, drove her 200 kilometers down a dirt road and across a river by ferry to a hospital. She was almost dead when they arrived. The surgeon there scolded the doctor for showing up with someone so sick without warning. They performed a cesarian and presented her with a four-pound baby girl.

But the little girl had a mother who had given up on life. She couldn't sit up, couldn't eat, couldn't name her child and had neither the milk nor the energy to feed her. She didn't even know where she was. Neither, in fact, did her family. She was just fading away and didn't care. The baby developed a lung infection and started to choke on her own secretions. Elizete developed a fever. All she could do was cry, and all the baby could do was whimper. The doctor stayed with her for days and told the hospital he would pay her expenses. After a few days he realized that he couldn't save her. She was going to have to save her self. He grabbed her by both shoulders and shook her violently, screaming that if she wanted to die, she could go ahead and die, but he was going to save the baby. The baby was fighting for her life. Is that what she wanted, to give up and leave her baby fighting for her own life?

It shook her to her core. She realized she had to live, and slowly she began to recover. She named the baby Valquíria, after a Norse warrior goddess. And after she got home, she realized she had to take charge of her life. She divorced her husband, worked her way through college, then did post-graduate work in herbal remedies and oriental massage therapy. She taught yoga for a while and got involved in community work again.

And the community needed work. In the 1980s, Terra Nova do Norte was just rising up from the mud when gold was discovered. A single sluice could sift over a kilo in a day. Peasants poured in, especially from Brazil's impoverished northeast region. These were non-people born without benefit of birth certificate, people never blessed with a pair of shoes, illiterates who had no idea where the trucks were taking them except that it was the place with the gold. The consequent mining camps were as lawless and ruthless as the worst of the American gold rush camps. Murders were more frequent than births. Peixoto de Azevedo, just to the north of Terra Nova, became a decadent camp town of tents and shacks, mud and mercury, booze and prostitutes, malaria and hepatitis, casual homicide over nuggets and love. No one knows how many people lived there, but it's widely said that 6,000 of them were prostitutes. The only law was the "Law of the .38." The police didn't do much about the nightly killings except go around town with a mule cart to pick up the bodies and dump them into a hole or a river. A priest posted photos of the dead in case anyone could identify them. Nobody knew anybody's real name.

A man in Terra Nova today, known simply as Chalera, was big in the gold camps. He knew how to find it. One of his sluices produced half a kilo in an hour. Once he paid someone half a kilo of gold for a small plot of land. He soon pulled three kilos from it. He loved finding gold, yet he didn't love money. He was generous and fun-loving, one of few people in the camps who didn't have any enemies. But he was surrounded by violence. He knew of divers who were murdered while sucking up mud from the bottom of the river. They wore divers suits with a helmet and an air hose up to the surface. After they'd brought up enough gold, the guys on the boat would cut off his air supply so they could keep his share of the gold. He saw a man stab his wife and throw her out a window. He was there when another woman, drunk and pregnant, told her husband it wasn't necessarily his baby. He drew his gun and shot her in the gut. He then gave her a hug and walked away, never to be seen again. Chalera and others tried to save her, wrapped her in a hammock and took her in a truck to a doctor, asked him to at least save the baby, who was visibly kicking. The doctor said he couldn't or he might lose his license.

Chalera liked to hire men from Maranhão, a state in northeast Brazil, on the coast just south of the Amazon. They were dumb but tough, a breed of black crossed with Indian. He knew of one man who had a bad case of malaria. He took five malaria pills and washed it down with cachaça, the Brazilian sugar cane rum. He never had another problem with malaria.

Today, Chalera is basically penniless, but he doesn't care. Rich or poor, hot or cold, rain or shine, up or down, it's all the same to him. He says he wouldn't have the courage to do it again — not that he could. Brazil's environmental protection agency has clamped down on rogue mines, and the easy gold is gone.

Back in the 80s, Paulo Pinheiro, desperate for cash, went off to try his luck at a mining camp. He was one of those people who just couldn't find gold. He came back with nothing but malaria. He made his money — enough to put his kids through college — selling garden produce directly to miners. Not much else paid off. Sales to Coopercana never added up, and the big crops he planted never did well. He tried everything. Corn. Rice. Guaraná. Coffee. Cotton. The thin soil yielded little. About the only thing that generated cash was cattle. Pretty soon that's all he and everyone else produced. The forest was gone, the rains diminishing, rivers getting lower, springs drying up. Grass was about all that would grow outside of a garden, and every year the pastures spent less time green and more time dry. He still raises cattle on a plot of about 90 hectares, but he regrets what he did to the forest.

Terra Nova do Norte itself has also moved up and settled down. Tall, broad mango trees shade the parallel lanes of Avenida Schwantes and its several speed bumps. The town has a branch of Banco do Brasil, a supermarket, boutiques, pharmacies, a cobbler, an ice cream shop with the exotic flavors of local fruits, a juice shop with even more flavors, a stationary store that sells fishing supplies, a little department store with mattresses leaning against the front wall, five restaurants, a nice church, three hotels, a place with computers and internet access, a hospital, and decent schools. People drive into town for concerts and farmers markets at the central plaza. Elections don't necessarily involve murder. The municipal government still tends to serve the interests of elected officials, but hey, it's Brazil.

Glenn Alan Cheney

Chapter Seven

Capitalismo

In Amazonia the worst of capitalism and free enterprise meets the bastion of nature, the last that nature has to offer. The grotesque mess and utter uselessness of gold mining, the extraction or destruction of natural resources, the loss of whatever has no mass market value right now, the lack of planning by anything other than the market, the absolute exploitation of people held in slavery, the development of unsustainable business at the cost of future business, the upward concentration of capital and consequent loss of power where there's no capital, the abuse of nature for the sake of excessive consumption, the imbalance of man and nature, the struggle of good and evil — it's all here, and the flames of it turn the sky pink.

It used to turn the sky dark. Epifânia Vuaden, the eco-agronomist, tells me of a time just four years ago when you could barely see across the street. That smoke was from a fire 325 km away.

I woke up one morning and noticed the sky especially pink. There was also a smell of burning garbage in the air. People will do that, just pile their week's garbage — the food scraps, the disposable diapers, the plastic bottles, everything — in the street and light it and let it smolder for a day or two. By mid-morning I learned that the smell wasn't garbage. It was the town of Marcelândia, 60 km to the south. It was on fire. It apparently started as arson intended for an acampamento of landless people. Now the TV says a hundred houses and four lumber mills have gone up in flames.

*   *   *

Dr. Fiorelo Picoli, a professor at Mato Grosso State University, has written extensively on the dark side of capitalism and its effects on Mato Grosso. He says the military government pushed for the settlement of the Amazon region for several reasons. It wanted to relieve some of the socio-economic pressures in the cities, where millions had migrated into horrific slums. It wanted to populate an area it saw as vulnerable to foreign invasion and occupation if no one was living there. It also believed that settlement would eventually contribute to the gross national product by exploiting more of the Brazilian territory.

Picoli interprets the history of the region, or the "development" (his air quotes) of the region, as a series of people taken from the land. First went the Indians so that the military could use the land for training. In the north of Mato Grosso, they were slaughtered secretly by the military or moved forcibly to reservations. In some cases, tribes were moved from a place where they had been inconvenient to someone who wanted the forest for the trees. The tribes typically ended up in a different environment where they had no knowledge of the plants and animals and thus no way to use nature for their survival.

Once the government decided to settle the area, the military moved out and the timber people moved in. Once most of the trees were gone, the timber people left. The gold prospectors came in. Their devastation of the land was grotesque, leaving it unsuitable for planting anything at all. The mining process was generally a process of sucking up mud from the bottom of rivers or spraying river water onto land to make mud that could be channeled down sluices. Untold tons of mercury, used to separate gold from other materials, went into rivers and the air. After ten or fifteen years, the gold got scarcer and government managed to stop a lot of the mining. The miners left. Then the cattle ranchers moved in, removed or burned any trees that remained, burned planted grass, put fencing around their county-sized pastures, and began the methodical process of sending the last of the soil's nutrients up in smoke.

When cattle ranching becomes unviable, the ranchers will leave. At that point, there won't be much left to sustain human life.

The Catholic Church, he says, has been of little help. For the most part, its has simply offered a salve to suffering people. Injustices were their due. Malaria would get them into heaven. Render unto Caesar what is Caesar's. While it was obvious that people were being exploited and that the land was being ruined beyond use, he says, the Church did nothing but preach the love of Jesus. The evangelicals were even worse, talking about God but not giving even lip service to the grave and ubiquitous social problems. Although Sister Leonora and the CPT get a little moral support from some factions of the Church, many simply disregard her existence. He says she is an "isolated symbol of resistance."

Picoli is as cynical and pessimistic as anyone, but he detects just a bit of change. Something's happening, he says. In recent years, he's seen 50 or so people arrested by federal police. Among them have been people from the ranks of what he and others call organized crime, the conspiring, self-serving, criminal network of politicians, police, and big landowners.

Mato Grosso, however, is still teetering on a pre-

Typical locally built farm car

carious line between civility and lawlessness. The ranchers are pushing for a federal law that would legally give them ownership of the land they claim, erasing all the hopes of land reform, justifying all the killing, beating, stealing, threatening, stonewalling, fraud, and the little homemade bomb somebody tucked under Leonora's car in January of 2011, too small to kill her but big enough to ruin a tire.

Promised Land

Glenn Alan Cheney

Chapter Eight

Slavery

There really are slaves in Brazil — uncountable thousands of them. The very nature of the phenomenon makes it hard to estimate their numbers. The enslavement tends to take place in remote places where the slaves cannot be seen and from which they cannot easily flee. The slaves themselves are always deeply ignorant people, illiterate and uninformed, peasants who often have no idea that they are slaves. They only know they are not being paid. They may be without documentation certifying their existence, so their disappearance may never be noted. They tend to come from far away, hired with promises of employment and trucked hundreds of miles to a place they never heard of. Their families may not expect them back — may, in fact, have sold them — and they have no friends besides the people working beside them.

The enslavement is often based on the honor of the slave. Typically a middleman, known as a gato — a cat — hires men, women, and children for employment in another state. They are typically people who have zero income and little hope of gaining any. They tend to come from Brazil's impoverished and often parched northeast region, the states of Pernambuco, Rio Grande do Norte, Ceará, Maranhão, Piau-i. They end up in the states of the Amazon region, states of little law: Pará, Mato Grosso, Amazonas, Acre. These people have little or no idea of their rights and little expectation of any more than fraction of the minimum wage, which itself is too little to live on.

As one man in an *acampamento* told me, slavery has not been abolished. it has simply been modernized. The only chains needed are those of ignorance, poverty, and fear. Greed is sufficient whip.

The "job" is usually at a cane plantation, a cattle farm, or at a forest in the process of being cleared for timber and pasture. Typically the "employer" will put the people to work under miserable conditions. They may sleep on the ground, perhaps without shelter. Their food — at best a hash of rice and beans — may arrive in a bucket. Their "supervisors" are armed and brutal. When payday comes around, the workers are informed that they owe the employer for their food, the tools they've been using, their accommodations. The workers actually feel honor-bound to pay off their debts, but of course they never reach that point.

If they try to leave, they are threatened with death, perhaps  beaten. If they flee, they may have to walk scores of miles in bare feet, and if they are caught, they will certainly be beaten, quite likely killed. They may be released one day, perhaps even handed a bit of money — more than they arrived with but hardly enough to survive more than a day or two elsewhere. Once it's gone, they may well go back to where they know they at least get a little food.

I asked Leonora how people can tolerate slavery. Why don't they rise up or run off?

"They accept it," she says. "They see it as normal."

The slaves' ignorance may be so thorough that they are unaware that they are slaves. In fact, they may accept "employment" at the same place later since food in a bucket is better than no bucket and no food. Often young people have seen their parents live this way, so it seems only natural to accept similar non-paying employment. They may not even know the concept of slavery. They see it as their lot in life — not good but not escapable.

Part of Leonora's work, then, is simply to educate people. A calendar produced by the CPT hits at the most basic level of education. The image of field worker — identifiable as such by the hoe over his shoulder, not his healthy, clean-cut appearance — touches one of his eyes with a finger, the

gesture of watching out for unseen danger. The written message is "Keep your eyes open to not become a slave." Down at the bottom, below the twelve months and a list of agencies and phone numbers, is an explanation in oddly small print: "Don't be fooled by the promises of the gato. To oblige someone to work off debts is a crime. In case of doubts, find your union or any of these agencies. And open your eyes!"

Once a fourteen-year-old boy showed up in town. He had escaped enslavement but left behind his father, who had been killed. There were other slaves still there. Leonora informed all the proper authorities. Three years later, nothing had been done. The boy was kept in hiding for a long time and eventually sent back to his home in Maranhão before he could be eliminated as a witness.

Promised Land

Glenn Alan Cheney

Chapter Nine

The Way the World Ends

Like many towns in the region, Terra Nova do Norte finds itself at the development stage of the 19th century frontier while facing the 21st century disappearance of nature as a resource. I have the feeling that in Mato Grosso I am glimpsing a microcosmic view of the end of the world. This is how it will end: The last of the resources peter out. A minuscule sliver of society owns virtually all assets and exploits for itself the last that the earth has to offer. The poor huddle at the edges of highways, occupying the least space physically possible, consuming barely enough to sustain life. Earth's most abundant resources — land and water, the very stuff of the planet — are contaminated, depleted beyond use, or precious beyond the reach of all but a few. The air smells of smoke. Violence maintains the socio-economic status quo but is powerless to sustain a useable environment. The situation deteriorates toward an apocalyptic tipping point. Irreplaceable resources are gone. Nature falls back to the ecosystem of a desert. Planetary poverty erupts into violent conflict over the last of whatever's left, but the victors are merely the last to go down.

Soil near Terra Nova do Norte

Or maybe my imagination is getting carried away in a pessimistic direction. It tends to do that. I'm probably extrapolating too much from what I see in Mato Grosso. Still, though it might not happen to the whole world, it is certainly happening here, though the death spiral may still be a decade off.

A few people have come to understand that the forest must be maintained or replanted, but the rest think the enlightened idealists are communists or pot smokers. Ranchers routinely cut down every single tree for a pasture even though leaving a few for shade would increase growth of grass and production of beef. It seems they actually hate trees. When the mayor of Terra Nova, Manoel Freitas, took me to his 750 hectare ranch, treeless but for a narrow strip along a stream, he expressed pride in his accomplishment. When he bought it

in 1999, it was all forest. He gave me a wicked, ironic laugh
and said, "I am a destroyer!"

Manoel Freitas on his ranch.

It was Elizete Pinheiros who got Freitas elected in 1999.
Tired of corrupt and do-nothing governments, she started a
new political party, served as Freitas's campaign manager,
and later did the same for a state representative and state
senator. Elizete served as Freitas's chief-of-staff, then the
town's acting Secretary of Agriculture, then a sub-secretary
on environmental issues. As the de facto recreation director
of the town, she started an annual music festival. She started
an organization to clean up and protect the Rio da Esperança
— the River of Hope — that runs through town, its flow dwin-
dling each year.

Soon Freitas and the others in the party turned corrupt. Freitas started paving a road from town directly to his farm, and he began accumulating inexplicable wealth. In 2010 he wasn't up for reelection, but he demanded that Elizete work on the campaigns of candidates he supported. She refused and told him why. He told her he'd fire her if she didn't support his party. She didn't, and two days after the election, he weeded her out. She had to drop out of a Masters in Business Administration program she had begun, and she faced the dismal prospect of finding a decent job in a town with little employment above a menial level.

For the next three years Elizete had no choice but to aim for some long-term income by pursuing her dream of replanting some of the

Balsa seed pods.

forest that her father and other pioneers had cut down. Recognizing that the land needs shade and that families need to sustain themselves, she started a not-for-profit association of balsa growers, the Cooperativa de Productores de Pau de Balsa, or COPROMAB. Balsa is a new and high-profit crop. It's the raw material of more than model airplanes. It insulates high-speed trains and strengthens the blades of wind generators. The association recognizes the danger of a monoculture forest. The plan is for farmers to reforest the required portion of their land, in some cases using the fast-growing balsa to shade seedlings of trees that will remain unharvested. It's a good alternative for small family farms because it yields more money per hectare than cattle. The only problem is that the seedlings need intense care for a couple of years, and the increasingly long dry season is hard on them. Theoretically, under ideal conditions, half the trees can be harvested after three years, the rest a few years later. The hectare that could support one head of cattle yields balsa worth tens of thousands of dollars.

"We need to recognize that people live here," Elizete

Farmer in his family's new balsa stand.

says. "To have a sustainable economy we need to balance the need for crops and the need for forest. We need both."

With money from investors and Elizete's own unremunerated sweat-equity, the association planted several hectares as a pilot project to test for ideal growing conditions. Her husband developed remarkably beautiful furniture and decor accessories of balsa. The association participated in trade shows. But it was hard to sell in Mato Grosso and expensive to ship to São Paulo. Unemployment was her present, but balsa was her future. She was poor and sinking into debt, but as soon as her balsa grew to marketable size, she would be all set, and as soon as Mato Grosso saw that trees were more profitable than cattle, the land just might start to be saved.

Chapter Ten

Three Kinds of Farmer

L eonora wanted to show me what can be done with land in
the right hands, so she took me to the farm of Ari Angelo
Piccini. Piccini came to Mato Grosso and managed to tame it
without hurting people or the land. He moved to the region in
1983 and bought his current farm twenty years ago. He really
owns his land — as opposed to squatting on it for as long as
he can — so he really cares for it. It's a fruit farm. He grows
noni, aracá, marumbá, gravatá, cupuaçu, two kinds of tanger-
ine, atimoia, bacala, taperabá, araca, jackfruit, pitamba, pi-
tanga, buriti, murici, ouvaia, acerola, graviola, açai, tamarind, mango, limes, passionfruit, and melons. He also raises
some cattle, pigs, and chickens. This is quite an accomplish-

ment. No one else in the region manages to grow so much of so many fruits, and he does it without chemical fertilizers. To keep ants from stripping every leaf from every tree, which they are certainly eager to do, he hangs little pots of poisoned

sugar water on the trees — enough to kill enough, albeit not all. To snag the bugs of the night, he puts little lights over pans of used motor oil. He irrigates with little sprinkles that throw water no farther than needed. To conserve his water table, he's preserving what forest is still growing on his land, and he's planting more. He plants "pig beans" to fix his soil, which needs all the help it can get. He uses every scrap of organic material from his fruit trees as compost or mulch. He doesn't know what to do about parrots. They come in hordes that can gnaw the limes off a tree in no time at all.

When he first arrived in Terra Nova, as he tested the strange, tropical land, he tried rice. He tried corn. It never panned out. He had better luck with tropical fruits. The problem was how to get them to markets a thousand miles away. The solutionw as to process them into frozen pulp that could be made into juice. He packs it into little plastic bags and freezes them. He and two sons do all the field work, an amazing feat of coordinating plantings, pruning, picking, and all the other steps involved in growing so many different types of fruit. In all likelihood the farm — the land so carefully, lovingly sustained and improved — will belong to the sons.

On Sundays the family rests. They usually have a gaucho-style barbecue under the mango tree that Piccini planted when he bought the place 20 years ago. The shade today is sixty feet across.

*   *   *

Leonora also takes me to see some farmers of another sort, the sort that doesn't own land. They live at a small acampamento just south of Terra Nova. It's about a kilometer long, 25-45 meters wide, a row of shacks between BR-163 and a barbed wire fence. INCRA has agreed to buy the ranch on the other side of the fence for redistribution, and the farmer has agreed to sell. But it's a complicated transaction. In the latest development, the federal forestry agency has to approve that land for inhabitation and agriculture rather than forest. The fact that the forest is gone apparently doesn't figure in. Until this and other issues are resolved, the rancher continues to do his ranching, and 60 or 80 people continue to wait in their shacks. They've been there for seven years.

Most of the inhabitants of this humble sliver of the world are in town for a Saturday market. Sílvio and a handful of others maintain a presence. Sílvio, bright-eyed, fast-talking, shows us his seedlings. He has over 3,000 coffee plants in little black plastic sacks. He also has mango, *cajá, cupuaçu, bacaba* (a palm also known as the north-south palm because its fanned leaves point in those directions), *piqui, copaiba* (the sap of which is reputed to prevent and cure cancer), *abacaba, guarantã* (a slice of its trunk having the outline that might have been drawn by a kid with a wandering crayon), tamarind, breadfruit, *camu-camu*, flamboyant trees, red guava, white guava, *seringueiro* (rubber tree), *abelha jatai, jatauba, jabudicaba, gilô, maniotucum* (for heart of palm and little fruits that feed parrots and wild animals), a variety of peppers (*doce, cumari, bode, malagueta, cheiro*), herbs, greens, ferns, orchids, lemon grass, bush beans that can break up soil ruined by being stripped of nutrients and baked naked in the sun.

People have things planted all over the camp in all kinds of containers: food cans, paint cans, soda bottles, crates, curved bark, plastic tubs, old juice pitchers, tires, a section of a tire, a cracked tea pot. The containers sit on benches, hang from eaves, hold forth on walls — little pieces of farm perched everywhere. These people have done their planting. All they need is land for the plants. They are capitalists without the most fundamental capital, so they have to be socialists accepting food from the government, food they'd be more than happy to grow themselves.

Leonora takes me to yet another kind of farmer, farmers

who more or less own their land. They live at a pre-assentamento on the outskirts of the town of Claudia on the side of BR-163. The people there are slightly settled in, not with permanent houses but with a few fruit trees and gardens planted. They offer seedlings for sale, and some of the women do some

weaving. Leonora left me there while she went into Sinop, a regional city, to get information about a dam project that's planned for the Rio Teles Pires. The dam is one of five planned for that river. Three more are planned for the next river downstream, the Tapajós, which flows into the Amazon at Santarém. The dams will make the rivers navigable, a death warrant for the remainder of the rainforest in the region. A river route to the Amazon will make it cheaper to send beef and soy to the international market, cheaper to import fertilizer and pesticides, and more profitable to replace forest with field.

The dams go hand in hand with BR-163 to doom the region to ecological disaster. The highway goes north 900 km to the Amazon, and south 700 km to Cuiabá. From Cuiabá, the nearest port, Santos, is 2,200 km away. The route south is paved. The route north is just mud, all but impassable during much of the year. It takes weeks to get to the Amazon, but a project to pave the highway to the north is underway. If the project manages to reach completion, the trip will be able to be made in a couple of days. Like dammed rivers, BR-163 will serve exporters. The few beneficiaries will be corporations, not family farms. To a corporation, a forest has no value unless cut down. A family farm has no need to export anything, little or no use for imported fertilizers and pesticides. The billions spent on the highway and the dams will not benefit them in the least.

The completion of the highway and the many dams are

by no means a sure thing. Brazil has a tendency to start big projects, only to abandon them for lack of funding or political follow-through. The Mundurucu Indians along the

Office at the acampamento.

Tapajós are struggling to resist the dams, and they have the Brazilian constitution to back them up. Opposing them with terrifying efficiency is a political block known as *ruralistas,* who are dedicated to developing the Amazon region without concern for the environment, Indians, or small family farms.

In this pre-assentamento, about a hundred people live on plots they've been assigned, though they still lack deeds. INCRA bought the land years ago, but now former owners and other claimants are trying to undo or redo the deal. The issue's tied up in the courts, so nothing moves.

Meanwhile, the people living there are planting fruit trees with the hope that they will get to pick the fruit. Their crude houses seem a little more permanent than the huts of acampamentos. I hang out with Valdemar Nunes all day. He and his

wife Rita are one of the two families that remain from the original encampment of eight years ago. He plants a few things but is a little

Valdemar and Rita

too old for full-fledged farming. For lunch, Rita prepares us a savory chicken dish worthy of a fine restaurant. A neighbor shows up with a rare luxury: a liter of ice in an old soda bottle. He has a freezer because he has electricity. He built an ingenious waterwheel that turns a little generator down at a creek. It's an ingenious mechanism that involved not only precision in the working with wood but complicated calculations of RPMs as the energy transfers from axles to chains to gears to finally turn the generator at precisely the right speed. He takes me to his little house to for some nice, cold lemonade.

He shows me the boa constrictor he decapitated just outside of his yard. It had been eating his chickens. Now flies are eating the boa constrictor.

Meanwhile, Valdemar seems unconcerned about the smoke boiling up from behind a hill near his house. It's a brush fire approaching the camp. Most of the men are over there trying to put it out, a dicey, touch-and-go task for men in flip-flop sandals. The fire was set by somebody on a motorcycle. The men are reluctant to call the fire department because they know the local government would just as soon see the camp burn. They're also pretty sure they'd get blamed for starting the fire. Late in the afternoon Leonora shows up bearing bad news. She calls everyone — everyone who isn't fighting the brush fire — to a meeting area, a set of benches under a thatched roof. She has bad news. the Sinop dam planned for the Teles Pires will eventually swamp the land that the campers have been promised. Obviously this would not happen in

time to put the brush fire out. Since the government will have to compensate anyone who loses land to the new lake, it's unlikely to hand over deeds. Why give out land only to have to buy it back? So everyone's been camping there for years and now will have land for barely enough time to take fruit from the trees they have planted.

Promised Land

Chapter Eleven

One Big Problem

If Sister Leonora seems to have her fingers in many pies, it's because she sees them as all one pie — the slavery, the poverty, the land misdistribution, the environmental collapse, the corruption of government, banks, unions, and police, and the violence. It's all one big problem that could be solved by one big solution: distributing land among people who live on it and take care of it. Family farms feed more people than cattle ranches, and the food stays local. Families are better stewards of the land because they live on it for generations. Better care of the land and its natural forests prevents the disappearance of streams, springs, and rain. Family farms don't keep slaves. Gardens don't need the agrotoxins that vast monocultures require. Small farmers don't buy politicians with anything but a lot of small votes.

Underlying the whole problem is capitalism and its evil instigator, greed. Leonora sees that economic system as dysfunctional. She has a better idea — solidarity economics.

The concept is that of capitalism with the rug pulled out from under it. Instead of rallying to the cause of greed, solidarity economics is a compassionate capitalism based on community and cooperation. It doesn't need to overthrow capitalism. It works in capitalism's nooks and shadows. It fits right in. And anybody can do it.

I earn certification in solidarity economics in two days flat at a little seminar that Leonora organized. Professors and practitioners meet with a few dozen disciples. I recognize some of them from acampamentos I'd visited. Others are college and high school students. In a Kumbaya ambience we break for periods of song, a prayer, lunch in a cafeteria, siestas in the dorm. Everyone drinks water from the same few jelly glasses at the water fountain. We write and act out pageants of righteous lower-class life depicting solidarity economics in action. We learn that we don't need to depend on a big company for a job. We can create our own. We don't need a lot of capital or a designated boss. We're reminded that profit isn't the only purpose of an enterprise.

With solidarity economics Sister Leonora aims to convert the soul of capitalism from the persuasions of greed to the possibilities of cooperation. At no point does she link  this to the precepts of Christianity. Nor does she drag God and Gospel into her meetings with politicians, technicians, attorneys, peasants, working women, the landless, the rich and the wicked. If they can't see Jesus in this, then there's no explaining it to them. She applies logic and the law, and she does it with as much love as she can muster in the face of greed. It works slowly, but she can claim to be getting somewhere. If she weren't, nobody would be trying to kill her.

* * *

Sister Leonora is not in Mato Grosso to spread the Gospel. She's there to save people, not souls. And the people she wants to save are for the most part poor. She sees saving the poor and saving the land as synonymous.

Transferring the land to family farmers, she says, would

solve so many problems. It would reduce poverty, corruption, pollution, welfare, and violence. It would preserve nature, communities, water, dignity, self-sufficiency and sustainability. All of this would be possible if so much land weren't in the hands of so few rich people, the very people, Leonora says, who are causing all the problems.

Leonora was no fan of the Pope — Pope Benedict, at the time — and she's not too happy about the Church. Support from priests and bishops has been sporadic. There was money involved, so it gets complicated. The money — the big money — comes from the upper class, what Leonora calls their "dairy cow." Some hold that the Church should stick to religion, stay out of politics, and keep passing the plate. Others, like Leonora, see Christ calling them to social action.

So as soon as she gets time, Leonora's going to get to work on the Church, too. She wants to organize its active women and hold a general strike until the management changes a few rules. Women are running the Church, she says, and they can shut it down. And then they can change the power structure. She says the Church has been negligent in applying the potentials of its power. It could be doing so much to save people and their planet. It could overthrow tyrants, force corporations into submission, effect the equitable distribution of land, and otherwise resist civilization's hellbent urge to exterminate itself.

One evening, driving home from an acampamento, driving through an indigo dusk, I'm at the wheel, an eye in the rearview for anyone following, an eye ahead for bandits and potholes, I finally dare ask Leonora something I've wanted to know since I first met her. Did she believe God would protect her from the bullets of *pistoleiros*?

"*Não*," she says with a wag of her finger. "God has already done everything he's going to do."

"Does prayer work?"

"We shouldn't ask more or expect more from God," she says. "It's a question of expecting something from man. God did his part. His part doesn't fail. The problem is man's intervention in God's plan. Man ends up destroying what God built and what man has to preserve. It's hard to say what to expect of God. To me, God has carried out his plan perfectly. When will man wake up and let God's plan run so everybody has life and abundance?"

She sees the New Testament not as a path to personal tranquility but a call for struggle.

"It's hard to understand how an evangelical can be at peace," she says. "I could be at peace. I could retire, have a more tranquil life. But it's impossible to be tranquil when you see your brother humans suffering. Impossível."

She also says she's getting tired. By the middle of 2013, there had been no new *asentamentos*, no progress whatsoever. Sebastião "Chapeu Preto" Neves de Almeida was somewhere other than in prison. The new president, Dilma Rousseff, who had been annointed by President Lula, was delivering little that she had promised and changed nothing in Mato Grosso.

When the Brazilian congress passed a new Forest Code that made it possible for farmers to reduce the amount of forest they are supposed to preserve, Rousseff signed it into law. Within a year, the rate of deforestation across the Amazon region increased by 30 percent. Meanwhile, *ruralistas* proposed two amendments to the constitution were making their way through congress. One would allow congress to reduce the size of Indian reservations. The other would make it easier for farmers, miners, timber companies, dam builders, and other developers to use, if not actually take, Indian land for the sake of economic development. Leonora's efforts are proving pitifully ineffective against corporate pressure. Leonora moved from Terra Nova do Norte to Sinop so she could live in a residence with other sisters. She wasn't receiving so many death threats, but she says it's only because the ruralistas are confident that they are winning the battles and the war. She continues her struggle, but progress was so slow, the forces against her so huge, the people behind her poor and simple. The forest of Mato Grosso is all but gone. The cattle land is dying fast, and deforestation has picked up pace. It would seem the only hope is that when capitalism can wring nothing more from nature, the rich will leave, as they always do, and the meek will inherit their dry, dead earth.

Epilogue

In June of 2013, my article titled "Promised Land" — a short version of this book — appeared in Harper's magazine. I was very worried that the article would make its way to Brazil, with repercussions falling on Sister Leonora. Heedless of such a possibility, Leonora cast the article far and wide along with a translation. In August I received email from her. She said that the *acampados*, the Public Ministry, INCRA, the CPT, and the Advogado-Geral da União (an executive branch agency that defends constitutionality and the interests of the nation) were reaching an agreement to distribute land to 250 families, with other cases to continue in the courts. Forty-four family at the Novo Mundo *acampamento* families were already on their land, and 42 more were about to be placed. She said it wasn't easy, but that it seemed the article, which is to say international attention, was helping.

Promised Land

Glenn Alan Cheney

For Brazilian readers, the original article that appeared in the June 2013 issue of *Harper's Magazine* is appended here in Portuguese, translated by the author. All information in the article has been included in this book.

Para leitores brasileiros, o artigo original que apareceu na edição de junho de 2013 da revista *Harper's Magazine* é anexado aqui em português, traduzido pelo author. Todas as informações do artigo foram incluidas neste livro.

PROMISED LAND
Will Brazil's rural poor ever inherit the earth?
By Glenn Cheney

I'm sitting in the back seat thinking, *Nuns can't drive.* Or maybe it's just nuns with a lot on their minds. Or maybe it's just Sister Leonora Brunetto, bearing on her sixty-four-year-old shoulders the weight of slavery, kleptocracy, landlessness, lawless-

Glenn Cheney is the author of more than twenty books, including, most recently, Love and Death in the Kingdom of Swaziland.

ness, forest fires, hit squads, environmental devastation, and the ravages of capitalism. The year is 2010, and she's driving erratically down a ragged highway in the central Brazilian state of Mato Grosso. She speeds up, slows down, squints into the dark beyond the headlights, then remembers the rearview mirror, then remembers the accelerator.

Half the problem, I think, is Elizete Pinheiro, the woman sitting next to her. She's filling us in on the political misconduct in the nearby town of Terra Nova do Norte. Pinheiro works for the municipal government there, as coordinator of the environmental department, which means that she's knee-deep in a slurry of shady deals and embezzled funds. She hates it—

A boy aiming his slingshot at the *fazenda* across from the Cinco Estrelas encampment in northern Mato Grosso, where he and his family live. All photographs from April 2013 © Nadia Shira Cohen

Glenn Alan Cheney

From *Harper's Magazine,* June 2013

Terra Prometida

Será que pobre rural do Brasil nunca herdarão a terra?

E u estou sentado no banco de trás, pensando, Freiras não sabem dirigir. Ou talvez seja apenas freiras com muito em suas cabeça. Ou talvez seja apenas a irmã Leonora Brunetto, tendo em seus ombros de 64 anos o peso da escravidão, cleptocracia, falta de terra, a ilegalidade, os incêndios florestais, pistoleiros, devastação ambiental, e os estragos do capitalismo. No momento, ela está dirigindo de forma irregular por uma estrada irregular no estado central de Mato Grosso. Ela acelera, desacelera, aperta os olhos para o escuro além dos faróis, em seguida, lembra-se do espelho retrovisor, em seguida, lembra-se do acelerador.

Metade do problema, penso eu, é Elizete Pinheiro, a mulher sentada ao seu lado. Ela está nos informando na conduta política na vizinha cidade de Terra Nova do Norte. Pinheiro trabalha para o governo municipal lá, como coordenador das assuntos ambientais, o que significa que ela está atolado em uma pasta de negócios obscuros e fundos desviados. Ela odeia isso e quando ela fala, sua voz se eleva com indignação. Eu, também, teria dificuldade de dirigir.

Mas ela cala quando Leonora toca o espelho retrovisor e diz: "Eles estão nos seguindo." "Quem?"

"Pistoleiros".

Não importa o quão rápido ela vai, eles ficam a poucas centenas de metros atrás de nós. Eles estão com a gente, Leonora desde enchjamos o tanque em Alta Floresta, meia hora atrás. Nós ainda estamos uma hora a partir da próxima cidade. Entre aqui e ali, as casas são poucos, os carros raros, o céu escuro da noite com a fumaça da queima de pastagens. É um bom lugar para um hit. Não há sinal de telefone celular, mas isso pouco importa, já que não há ninguém para chamar. Certamente não a polícia. Os pistoleiros no carro atrás de nós provavelmente estão policiais fora de serviço no momento, mas em conluio com seus colegas no serviço.

Leonora bate os freios com força quando nos viramos para a ponte sobre o Rio Teles Pires. É um período especialmente difícil de estreito, concreto craterado, uma centena de metros de comprimento. O carro atrás de nós de repente fica em cima do nosso pára-choque, os faróis enchendo o nosso carro e inundando o rosto de Leonora. Não há como voltar, como virar, nem manobrar. Só mais tarde é que Leonora nos dizer de seu medo de que este era o momento em que ela estava esperando nos últimos dez anos, o momento em que ela descobre ao certo o que Deus faz com os mortos.

Os pistoleiros permanecem em cima de nós como nós burburimos sobre a ponte, em seguida, caem para trás quando Leonora acelera o ppuco seu carro consegue Ela vira à direita para a estrada em direção a Terra Nova e desvia em torno de um caminhão com móveis empilhados e camponeses. Mais para frente da estrada é o pequeno restaurante onde almoçamos mais cedo no mesmo dia, gerido por uma família que a ama. A estrada desce para um trecho, em seguida, sobe- e o restaurante aparece. Leonora corta bruscamente para a esquerda, foge atrás de uma árvore, e apaga os farois. Meio minuto depois, um carro passa correndo. É um VW Gol azul-escuro.

"São eles", diz ela.

Um monte de gente quer Irmã Leonora morta. Mas muito mais, talvez milhares, tratam ela de Mãe. Este último grupo inclui agricultores marginalizados em acampamentos de beira de estrada, escravos fugitivos que se escondem na casa dela, ativistas de todos os matizes, e as mulheres que começaram pequenas empresas sob a tutela de Leonora. Este papel maternal deu-lhe, pelo menos, alguma medida de proteção. Cruel, ganancioso e ignorante como certas pessoas em Mato Grosso pode ser, eles sabem o que acontece quando uma pessoa mata a mãe de alguém.

Em um acampamento numa estrada de terra perto de Terra Nova, eu pedi alguns homens o que aconteceria se alguém matasse a Irmã Leonora. Já estava anoitecendo no acampamento ragítico, que os habitantes chamadam de Renascer. Sentamos em caixotes e troncos e cadeiras quebradas por trás da cabana remendada de um homem chamado Nico. Sob as estrelas feitas cor de rosas de fumo, passamos o chimarrão, a cuia bulboso de erva mate. Todo mundo bebeu do mesmo canmukdo de aço e fumando cigarros de tabaco preoa em retângulos de papel de caderno. Meninos jogam no chão, empurrando fotos de caminhões e buzinando um para o outro.

"Nada iria acontecer," Nico disse calmamente. "A irmã é a nossa esperança. Quando ela se foi, assim vai a nossa esperança. Ninguém vai fazer nada, da mesma forma que nunca tinha feito nada antes. "

Alguém discordou, dizendo que o assassinato de Leonora provocaria pessoas em ação. Os acampados finalmente se tornariam violentos.

A previsão de Nico é consistente com o passado. A história do pobre rural no Brasil é uma de resignação. Eles sofrem o abuso de posseiros ricos e a Polícia Militar como se fossem abençoados com uma capacidade infinita de absorver a punição. Uma razão para isso, diz um colega de Leonora, é que os coragosos são os primeiros a ser assassinado.

Em alguns casos, os pobres não são apenas abusadas, mas escravizados. Por lei, a escravidão foi proibida no Brasil desde 1888. Mas a prática era muito mais difundido aqui do que nos Estados Unidos. O Brasil importou, pelo menos, seis vezes o número de escravos africanos, como América do

Norte, então a idéia de usar trabalho forçado para o enriquec-
imento pessoal é mais arraigada na cultura. Trabalhadores
analfabetos ainda são regularmente levado a pensar que estão
em dívida com seus empregadores para alimentos e as ferra-
mentas que eles usam. Ou eles são forçados sob ameaça de
arma continuar trabalhando. Um homem no Renascer tinha
sido um escravo por doze anos. Ele dormia no chão e foi al-
imentado apenas o suficiente para se manter vivo. Uma vez
que ele fugiu, ele não fez nada para relatar dos seus captores,
não querendo arriscar a sua liberdade ou sua vida.

Mas, mesmo com os chamados bênçãos da liberdade,
os habitantes da Renascer têm sido espancados, roubados e
presos. Seis foram assassinados. Quando eles tentaram ocupar
um terreno que o governo federal havia prometido a eles bem
perto, um homem teve sua espinha quebrada. Outros foram
chicoteados com cerca de arame. Enquanto isso, escavadeiras
acabaram do acampamento. Em seguida, a polícia local levou
os restantes residentes em um caminhão e os largaram em
Terra Nova.

Foi somente com a chegada da Polícia Federal que os
acampados foram autorizados a estabelecer Renascer em seu
local atual. Mas essas forças não aparecem atoa. Eles não entram em disputas de terra sem algum tipo de liminar federal. E para obter essa injunção, um pessoa precisa de alguém
como Irmã Leonora ao seu lado, disposto a montar rebanho ao
longo de todo o processo.

Por enquanto, então, as pessoas em Renascer estão a salvo de expulsão. No entanto, eles se ressentem profundamente ter que viver em barracos em uma estreita faixa de terra em frente de de um Éden interminável de grama no outro lado da estrada.

"Não temos nada, e eles têm tudo", Nico me diz. Sendo eles os bovinos, brahmas gordas dentro cinqüenta metros da sua cabana. Eles têm 15.000 hectares, enquanto o campo tem cerca de cinco hectares. Os gados têm toda a comida que podem comer enquanto o campo vive de nutrição mínima. Eles recebem assistência médica, que as pessoas não recebem. Eles são protegidos pela polícia, e os moradores do acampamento são agredidos pela polícia.

Mas os animais também são vulneráveis, supervisionados por nada mais do que meia dúzia de caubois. Um pequeno grupo de camponeses poderia fazer um monte de danos. Eles poderiam fazer o rancho impossível de operar. Ninguém neste acampamento sugeriu tal ação, mas deve ter ocorrido a eles. Há, no entanto, dois obstáculos no caminho. Um deles seria as tratores consequentes, colunas quebradas, chicotadas, e tiros. O outro é uma freira de um metro e meio de altura chamada Mãe. Ela diz que não. E isso pode ser uma razão pela qual ninguém tem a matou.

O princípio da redistribuição agrária foi escrito na nova Constituição do Brasil, em 1988. Ela permite que o governo apropriar áreas improdutiva, com a compensação ao proprietário, e entregá-lo aos pequenos agricultores. Ela também manda a distribuição de terras que sempre pertenceram ao

Estado, mesmo que a terra é ocupada por posseiros. O programa é supervisionado pelo Instituto Nacional de Colonização e Reforma Agrária, ou INCRA.

Devido à sua localização remota no interior do Brasil, Mato Grosso ficou pouco habitado no século XX. Até hoje, tem uma das densidades populacionais mais baixas de qualquer estado brasileiro. Os primeiros europeus começaram a aparecer durante o início do século XVIII para explorar ouro na região, mas o estado permaneceu povoada em grande parte por tribos indígenas até os anos 1970, quando o governo federal começou a promover desenvolvimento. Desesperados para sobreviver e ansioso para ficar rico, os imigrantes de todo o Brasil queimamram a floresta e cercaram extensões de terra enormes, que agora suportam vários milhões de cabeças de gado, bem como campos extensos de algodão, soja e de arroz.

Mas a menos que a terra foi vendida especificamente a esses fazendeiros e agricultores, a terra ainda pertence ao Estado. Muitos milionários, alegando de possuir dezenas de milhares de hectares, são legalmente posseiros (grilheiros). Alguns conseguiram chegar registrar/legalizar a terra como o seu próprio, e títulos falsos voam em torno de Mato Grosso como tantos urubus flutando nas correntes de convecção. Com essa documentação frágil, grandes propriedades foram compradas, vendidas, subdivididas, mesmo hereditáriadas. E aqueles que tiraram a floresta tropical ou pensam que compraram um pedaço legítimo da terra não desistam fácil.

INCRA, por sua vez, move-se muito lentamente. Ela falta

pessoal e vontade política. É selado com uma burocracia terrível, e os títulos e documentos que manipula são complexas e muitas vezes comprometidas. Juízes e políticos, que podem ser grandes grilheiros, têm pouco incentivo para fazer o trabalho direito. Transferências de terras que poderiam ter sido concluídas em 60 dias ainda estão definhando depois de uma década.

Em uma ocasião, acompanho Leonora para o escritório do Incra em Colíder. Seu objetivo é motivar uma transferência que foi definhando há anos. Ela é cumprimentada calorosamente pela equipe esqueleto, que está gradualmente sendo apinhados por armários de arquivos.

O gerente parece sincero em seu desejo de resolver a questão e ficar livre dela. No entanto, ele leva meia hora para explicar todas as razões pelas quais ele não pode. Eles cortaram seu orçamento, nada é informatizado, os grilheiros estão apelando casos, outras pessoas estão reivindicando a terra, outras agências estão sentados em cima dos documentos, os tribunais têm de tomar decisões. O que ele não diz é que ninguém com poder, dinheiro ou terra não quer nada mudar.

Depois, na calçada do lado de fora do escritório, falamos com Valdir, um ativista sob a asa de Leonora, que vive em um Acampamento perto de de Nova Canaã, no norte do estado. Seu celular toca. A pessoa do outro lado, o seu número bloqueado, chama Valdir um cachorro sem vergonha e diz-lhe que este é o dia em que ele vai morrer. Ele adiciona um comentário bruto sobre Leonora antes de desligar.

No carro, no caminho de volta para a Terra Nova, Leonora me diz que "eles" grampiam seu telefone, bem como os telefones de todos que ela chama. Por "eles", ela significa os fazendeiros, a Polícia Militar, e, ela suspeita, a Agência Brasileira de Inteligência. Uma vez, eles atrapalharam a escuta e ela podia ouvir o que estava acontecendo do outro lado. Ela acha que foi a delegacia de polícia, porque ouviu os sons de alguém sendo espancado eram claramente audíveis no fundo.

Eles vigiam ela. Eles sabem que ela estava conversando com Valdir Fora do escritório INCRA. Eles sabem onde ela está acontecendo agora, e eles sabem quem está no carro com ela. Eles fazem essas ameaças, diz ela, porque eles sabem que estão perdendo.

Se o INCRA é tão adepto a arrastar os pés, como os acampamentos continuam se multiplicando? Aqui está o negócio. Primeiro, alguém faz uma pesquisa em um foro e identifica um pedaço de terra que sempre pertenceu ao Estado. Contanto que esta terra não é preservada como floresta, os cidadãos têm direito a um pedaço dele.

Em seguida, um grupo destes reclamantes se unem, geralmente sob os auspícios ou o Movimento dos Trabalhadores Rurais Sem Terra (MST) ou a Comissão Pastoral da Terra (CPT), com quem trabalha Leonora. Então, sem aviso, os acampados se estabelecem perto ou adjacente à propriedade que eles estão reivindicando. Desde a terra ao longo de rodovias sempre é propriedade do Estado, que é onde eles tendem a estabelecer sua colonia de algumas dezenas ou algumas centenas de pessoas em uma faixa de cascalho, com o asfalto de um lado e uma cerca de arame farpado no outro. A idéia é que, eventualmente, os posseiros ausentes serão ejetados da pastagem estatal e os acampados vai se assentam lá.

Muitas vezes, porém, eles permanecem no acostamento da rodovia, em casebres caindo aos pedaços que sufocassem e vazam chuva. Eles tiram sua água de poços, banham-se de baldes, cozinham em fornos a lenha de barro. Eles iluminam seus barracos com lâmpadas de querosene caseiros, apenas voltas de algodão pregardos em latas, as pequenas chamas enviando-se rabiscos pretos oleosas de fumaça. Os homens saem para procurar trabalho de campo. As mulheres mantem suas casas limpas, suas panelas e frigideiras espantosamente brilhante. Um ônibus escolar pega as crianças todas as manhãs e os traz eles para casa um pouco mais sábios.

Cada Acampamento elege líderes e toma decisões em conjunto, na forma de uma reunião numa cidade de Nova Inglaterra. O uso de drogas, prostituição e embriaguez são estritamente proibidos, eo campo pode votar para expulsar transgressores.

Algumas pessoas desistem. Alguns persistem por anos. De tempos em tempos, em uma explosão de raiva e frustração, um Acampamento transborda seus limites e se transforma em uma "Invasão", uma expansão sem licença em um pasto nas proximidades. Isto é geralmente seguido pela chegada da polícia local ou jagunços e um rápido despejo, uma ejeção. Então, aqueles que sobreviveram e decide ficar por aqui voltam ao Acampamento.

De vez em muito tempo, um juiz realmente concede alguns acampados permissão para ocupar as parcelas que eles alegaram. A emissão de ações, no entanto, pode levar anos como INCRA junta a documentação necessária. Assim, esta fase é chamada um pré-assentamento: um presettlement. Quanto tempo uma afirmação pode ser sustentada sem uma ação, ou por quanto tempo até que a ação realmente é emitido, depende de quanto tempo os advogados estão dispostos a contribuir, quanta pressão pode ser colocado no INCRA e os tribunais, e se os juízes morrem , se aposentam, ou são comprados. Em raras ocasiões, um assentamento é aprovado. Mas a maioria dos acampados em Mato Grasso permanecem no limbo por anos em um momento, com apenas o MST ou a CPT entre eles e a próxima expulsão.

No norte do Mato Grosso, a face da CPT é da Irmã Leonora: de olhos castanhos, levemente enrugada, rápida para sorrir. Em qualquer situação, a sua mensagem padrão é: Não desista. E em uma manhã de junho em 2010, seu objetivo é manter várias centenas de pessoas no Acampamento Cinco Estrelas, para eles de desistir. Para esse fim, ela conseguiu a comissão de direitos humanos do governo nacional para enviar uma equipe de Brasília.

A equipe, que pára durante a noite em Terra Nova, inclue um advogado, um psicólogo, um sociólogo, um técnico de segurança, e seu diretor. Eles vão visitar Cinco Estrelas, estudar a situação legal, e avaliar o impacto psicológico de viver sob ameaças diárias de morte. Então, na forma intemporal de tais comissões, eles vão concluir algo e escrever um relatório sobre o assunto.

Nosso comboio de quatro veículos sai de Terra Nova pouco depois do amanhecer, um oficial da Polícia Rodoviária Federal ao volante de cada carro. Eu não sei o com que o Brasil alimenta sua polícia rodoviária, mas estes parecem muito maiores do que a Polícia local e todos os outros na cidade. Vestida com roupas camufladas e óculos escuros, cada um carrega algemas, uma arma de 9 mm semi-automática, uma faca tático amarrada na coxa, e munição suficiente para o combate sustentado. Eles parecem sombrias, alertos, desconfiados. Leonora anda no banco de trás. Eu começo a andar na frente com o condutor, Marco Antônio, que parece não gostar de mim. Eu tenho a sensação que eu sou uma complicação.

Cinco Estrelas, está perto de Novo Mundo, uma cidade 20 milhas da rota Brasil 163. Lá 180 famílias vivem em pequenas casas construídas de lâminas finas de fibra longa pregados em quadros de madeira. Os telhados são folhas de plástico com folhas de palmeiras jogadas sobre eles para fornecer um pouco de sombra, e para evitar o plástico de bater no vento. Os banheiros alpendres não têm telhados, mas as paredes são de tábuas grossas de madeira tropical.

A terra que foi prometido fica no outro lado da estrada, uma extensa propriedade chamada Fazenda Cinco Estrelas,. O posseiro atual, Osmar Rodrigues-Cunha, comprou-o de Sebastião Neves de Almeida (aka Chapeu Preto, ou "Black

Hat"), um pistoleiro conhecido que possui várias fazendas e administra várias outras, centenas de milhares de hectares no total. Os pistoeiros de Chapéu Preto tem caçado Irmã Leonora por períodos de até três dias. (Ele, por sua vez, acusou-a de enviar esquadrões de vida contra dele.) Ele foi preso em uma série de acusações, incluindo a escravidão e ocupação ilegal de terras, mas nunca ficou preso por qualquer período de tempo significativo.

Enquanto a Polícia Rodoviária descansa na sombra de uma cabana, uma dúzia de moradores se reúnem em um círculo. Irmã Leonora explica por que os visitantes têm vindo todo o caminho de Brasília. Então, em termos gráficos, simples, não-gramaticais, os moradores relatam os problemas com que se depararam. No início, eles se revezam, mas os testemunhos se confundem em elaborações de histórias uma em cima da outra.

Sete pessoas foram assassinadas. Um jovem foi concedida a permissão para pescar na propriedade privada e, em seguida, levou um tiro. Outra foi cortado na cabeça com machado e levou seis meses para morrer. Outro desapareceu. Quase todos os dias eles recebem ameaças telefonadas ou gritadas pela janela de um carro. Quando eles entram em Novo Mundo, jagunços perseguem-los. Suas motos são foradas da estrada. Seus filhos são perseguidos no ponto de ônibus. Suas lonas têm buracos de bala.

Em 21 de fevereiro de 2010, quatro meses antes de a comissão chegou, vinte e dois policiais militares e outros associados jogaram todo mundo do terreno, queimou o acampamento, e arrasou o que permaneceu. Os acampados fugiram 30 milhas até Guarantã do Norte e invadiram o escritório do Incra lá. Eles permaneceram lá por mais de um mês, exigindo a terra que tinha sido prometido há tanto tempo. Finalmente algum apoio federal veio, e todo mundo tinham que voltar e construir um outro acampamento. Os acampados estão com raiva, eles contam a comissão, porque não há nenhuma justificativa para o atraso na concessão de títulos de terras. O governo federal tem certeza de que é proprietária do imóvel ocupado ilegalmente pela Fazenda Cinco Estrelas,. INCRA tem manifestado a intenção de passar a terra para os acampados. Lotes familiares já foram definidos. Então, por que não acontece?

"Queremos uma resposta", diz um homem, palmas inclinado para o céu.

Outro oferece uma resposta: "A lei aqui é o dinheiro. Aqueles que têm o dinheiro determinam a lei ".

"Sete anos sob a lona é muito tempo", diz um homem velho.

"O que eles querem que façamos?", diz um homem mais jovem. "Ir para uma favela em algum lugar e viver roubando pessoas? Será que eles querem que fazemos garimpo de ouro? Será que eles querem que a gente criar gado pirata d e não pagar impostos sobre eles? "

Outra diz: "Nós não temos nenhuma segurança aqui. Eles podem vir a qualquer noite e matar todos nós. "

Outro tem uma piada: "Nós não estamos sem-terra. Temos terra. É sob as unhas. "

Em tons apologéticos, o advogado explica que sua comissão não controla o governo e não pode resolver os problemas da reforma agrária. "Nossa preocupação principal aqui", diz ele, "é mantê- lo vivo e continuar a luta."

Leonora diz-me mais tarde que o único objetivo da reunião foi mostrar alguma presença federal e dar às pessoas esperança suficiente para se segurar em um pouco mais. A presença federal também faz com que ela se sinta mais segura. Ela é menos provável de ser baleado se os fazendeiros acham que as repercussões poderiam chegar a Brasília.

No único restaurante decente de Terra Nova, ao lado da lagoa que fornece seu peixe, Irmã Leonora me diz que ela nunca iria se aventurar a meio quilômetro do centro da cidade, se eu não estivesse ai com ela. Não que ela pensa que eu sou prova de balas, mas um estrangeiro assassinado poderia de chamar a atenção internacional.

E quando ela me convida para ficar em um apartamento anexo à casa dela, eu entendi que ela queria um testemunho potencial. Então eu sai do Hotel Avenida, e lá estou eu, morando com uma freira. Temos refeições com sua companheira de casa, a Irmã Nilza. Eu faço parte da cozinha. Eu lavo pratos. Falamos muito. Ouço histórias de horror de padres, freiras, e camponeses assassinados, escravidão generalizada, a noite que sua casa foi invadida e roubada de todos os documentos dela enquanto ela se escondeu no banheiro no apartamento.

Ela conheceu a Irmã Dorothy Stang, uma norte-americana no estado do Pará, que foi assasinada em 2005, com a idade de setenta e três anos. Um dos culpados passou um pouco de tempo na prisão, foi libertado por um detalhe técnico, e, em seguida, foi preso novamente enquanto se aguardam decisões judiciais, e mais tarde liberado pdendente uma apelação. Outro ainda tem que ser julgado.

Uma semana depois de eu mudar, para a casa da Leonora a situação de Cinco Estrelas esquentou. Um juiz de Cuiabá está prestes a assinar um documento que será enviado ao Supremo Tribunal Federal em Brasília. Leonora vai ter que ir para o capital — uma viagem de ônibus de mais de 32 horas — para representar seu povo. Se ela não estiver lá, o caso, já com oito anos, vai se voltar até os tribunais estaduais, uma derrota catastrófica.

Dois homens de Cinco Estrelas venham para a casa. Leonora dá-lhes instruções firmes. Assim que o juiz da Suprema Corte assina o papel, o Acampamento tem que passar para a propriedade do Chapeu Preto no outro lado da estrada. Todo mundo lá sabe onde fica o seu lote de terra. Eles tem que construir rapidamente abrigos e iniciar o plantio. Eles estão a ficar fora da área de floresta reservada. Estar alerta. Formar grupos e ficar juntos.

"Pelo amor de Deus", diz ela, "não tocar em qualquer equipamento da fazenda que ainda está lá. Assente-se perto da casa principal, mas não ir para dentro. Certifique-se que todos sabem o que fazer e o que não fazer. Sem erros ou perdemos tudo. "

Naquela noite, ela recebe um telefonema da polícia local. Ela tem que fugir para fora da cidade pela manhã porque alguém está vindo para matá-la, a fim de evitar sua viagem a Brasília. Irmã Nilza tem que desaparecer também. E ela deve mandar aquele estrangeiro fora de sua casa, porque ela sabe quem ele realmente é. Então, eu volto ao Hotel Avenida, e para a próxima semana ninguém sabe onde Leonora é. Em seguida, ela aparece. O juiz em Cuiabá não conseguiu assinar o documento. Cinco Estrelas, ela me diz, está em pé de guerra.

A Comissão Pastoral da Terra cresceu especialmente ativa em Mato Grosso na década de 1990, quando a taxa de desmatamento aumentou. Os gananciosos já tinha explorado tudo o que poderia ter em suas mãos: primeira ouro, então a madeira, então a camada fina de solo permanecendo no topo do cascalho que está subjacente a maior parte do bioma amazônico. A floresta, no entanto, levou mais tempo a se esgotar, e ainda está sendo queimadas e derrubadas para dar mais espaço para o gado e a soja.

Algumas pessoas passaram a entender que a floresta deve ser mantida ou replantada, mas o resto acha que esses idealistas são comunistas e maconheiros. Fazendeiros rotineiramente cortam cada árvore num pasto, embora diexar um pouco de sombra iria aumentar o crescimento da grama e, portanto, a produção de carne bovina. Parece que eles realmente odeiam árvores. Quando o prefeito de Terra Nova, Manoel Freitas, me levou para sua fazenda de 1.850 hectares, que estava coberta de floresta apenas uma década atrás, ele expressou com orgulho que ele tinha arrancado a vegetação original. A propriedade era agora sem árvores, com exceção de uma faixa estreita ao longo de um riacho. Freitas deu-me uma risada irônica e disse: "Eu sou um destruidor!"

Essa economia, com base no roubo da natureza, é uma das formas mais degradantes do capitalismo. Pouco capital é investido. A fazenda, por exemplo, requer um pouco mais do que um rebanho e uma cerca. E aquele investimento, e o retorno, fluxa diretamente para fora da região.

Funciona assim: Precisa de um hectare de capim para alimentar uma cabeça de gado. A pastagem de 25 mil hectares produz uma grande quantidade de carne. Mas a carne é exportada e os lucros vão para um rico grilheiro ausente. Toda a empresa emprega apenas um punhado de trabalhadores. Durante a estação seca, que costumava ser de junho e julho mas agora se estende de maio a outubro — os fazendeiros queimam os campos para colocar um pouco de nutrientes de volta ao solo. Mas o ciclo de nutrientes, também, está sujeito a retornos decrescentes e, eventualmente, a grama pára de crescer. Quando a vegetação desaparece, os córregos e nascentes secam. Quando este processo não consegue tirar mais nada da terra, o rico vai sair e os humildes herdarão suas parcelas seca e desolada.

Este cenário não é um pesadelo distante e distopio. Isso já está acontecendo. A agrônoma Epifânia Rita Vuaden dá a região mais cinco ou dez anos. "A ficha caiu", diz ela. "Terra Nova já perdeu cinqüenta e seis nascentes. Algumas áreas não podem ser cultivados mais, e as pessoas acabam abandonado a sua terra. A terra está morta. "

Ela conhece pessoas de vinte anos de idade que nunca viram uma floresta. Quando seus pais eram daquelaidade, não havia nada aqui além de floresta.

Em colaboração com a Irmã Leonora e uma série de organizações sociais, Vuaden está lançando um projeto para começar a reflorestar a área. Por lei, os proprietários devem manter 80 por cento de sua propriedade em estado natural com mata nativa. Praticamente ninguém em Mato Grosso obedece o regulamento, e para ser justo, é irrealista esperar que eles façam isso. Se os

agricultores do Meio-Oeste americano deixar 80 por cento de suas terras voltar ao seu ecossistema natural, os Estados Unidos não teriam tanta comida.

Vuaden diz que o hectare de floresta produz mais benefícios econômicos — nozes, frutas, madeira — que uma cabedça única de gado que exige a mesma terra para pastagem. Mas, enquanto apenas um punhado de pessoas podem cuidar de milhares de hectares de pasto, a colheita da floresta é mais trabalhoso. Um senhor ausente em São Paulo não pode facilmente dirigir uma tal operação de longe. É um trabalho para um agricultor familiar com 250 hectares de terra, numa escala que permitiria aos agricultores para manter 80 por cento de floresta, com o resto dedicado a um jardim, um pequeno campo de culturas de rendimento, e uns dois ou tres leiteiras. A fazenda de 50 hectares, que destrói o meio ambiente da região sem devolver um centavo para seus habitantes, em vez disso poderia suportar 500 fazendas familiares.

Essa transformação, que contraria quase todos os interesses de dinheiro em Mato Grosso, não acontecerá sem uma luta. Ele vai exigir tempo e um nível quase desumano de paciência. Enquanto isso, Vuaden e seus colegas criaram o Projeto Semente, que paga as pessoas para trazer sementes nativas para um depósito em Terra Nova. Muitos dos coletores de sementes são os trabalhadores rurais que conhecem a floresta, tem tempo para procurar as sementes, e podem usar o dinheiro. O projeto, em seguida, mistura-se uma muvuca, uma mistura cuidadosamente formulada de sementes. Alguns vão brotar cedo e oferecer algo que pode ser colhida relativamente breve, de milho, por exemplo. Esse crescimento inicial, em seguida, produz sombra de árvores de crescimento rápido, como a balsa e pinheiro, que podem ser colhidas dentro de poucos anos. E essa sombra apoiará árvores de crescimento lento.

Uma vez chega a estação da chuva, a muvuca fica plantada em manchas cuidadosamente espaçados, cada um um metro quadrado e alguns centímetros de profundidade. O resultado: uma floresta tropical nascente. Este novo crescimento deve ser desbastado de vez em quando, mas fora isso, fica de piloto automático. O plano é plantar 220 toneladas de sementes de cerca de 3.000 hectares.

Leonora, como Vuaden, reconhece a utilidade da livre iniciativa. O que ela se opor é a ganância, na base do capitalismo. Ela tem uma idéia melhor: economia solidária, uma forma não-cruel do capitalismo que pode prosperar nos recantos e sombras do sistema atual. A economia solidária toma a forma de cooperativos, entidades sem fins lucrativos, vizinhos ou amigos formando microempresas, e as associações de empresários locais que decidiram que a melhoria da comunidade é do interesse de todos.

De vez em quando, a Leonora organiza seminários de dois dias sobre economia solidária, um dos quais eu participei em Colíder. Entre as duas dezenas de participantes, reconheço várias pessoas dos acampamentos que eu visitei. Outros são estudantes da faculdade ou colégios. Nós descansamos por períodos de canção, uma oração, o almoço no refeitório, sestas no dormitório. Todo mundo bebe a água de os mesmos jarras de geléia na fonte de água. Nós escrevemos e fazemosdramas teatricas sobre vidas justiceiras da classe baixa representando economia solidária em ação. É tudo descaradamente melosas e amigaveis,, até mesmo um pouco bobo. Mas nas mãos de Leonora, parece uma maneira perfeita para ensinar negócio para as pessoas simples, com bons corações e quase nada de experiência empresarial.

Leonora me leva para um Acampamento ao lado de Brasil Route 163. As pessoas de lá tem plantado uma verdadeira fazenda em sacos plásticos, latas de tinta, pneus velhos, um bule de chá quebrado, e qualquer outra coisa que irá segurar o solo. Um homem energético de olhos brilhante, chamado Sílvio, me mostra dezenas de mudas que ele vai plantar tão logo ele recebe o seu pedaço de terra. Metade dessas frutíferas eu nunca ouvi falar, entre eles cajá, cupuaçu, bacaba, camu camu, jataí, jabuticaba, fruta pão. A terra prometida (em todos os sentidos da frase) está no outro lado de uma cerca de arame farpado, já comprado de um fazendeiro pela Incra e aprovado para redistribuição, enquanto se aguarda a confirmação de que ele pode ser usado para a agricultura, em vez de florestamento.

No caminho para casa, dirigindo por um entardecer índigo, eu no volante, de olho no retrovisor para quem pode ser atrás, um olho à frente para bandidos e buracos, eu finalmente ouso perguntar Leonora algo que eu queria saber desde que eu a conheci . Será que ela acredita que Deus iria protegê-la das balas de pistoleiros?

"Nao," ela diz com um abanar de seu dedo. "Deus já fez tudo o que ele vai fazer."

"Será que a oração funciona?"

"Nós não devemos pedir mais nada de Deus. A questão não é se esperar qualquer coisa dele. É uma questão de esperar alguma coisa do homem. Deus já fez a sua parte. Agora o homem está fazendo uma bagunça de tudo".

A bagunça em Mato Grosso, diz ela, é a culpa dos ricos. A concentração de recursos naturais em tão poucas mãos é a causa fundamental da miséria, corrupção e devastação ambiental. A única solução possível é a distribuição de terras para os agricultores familiares.

"Esse é o plano de Deus", diz ela. "Isso é o que ele quer para nós."

E isso é o que ela está trabalhando. Ela não está fugindo de pistoleiros e cutucando burocratas para difundir o Evangelho ou salvar almas. Ela está tentando salvar a terra e seu povo, e eu ouço essas palavras — a terra e o povo — de seus lábios muito mais do que eu ouço Deus.

"E o novo papa?" Eu pergunto, referindo-me a Bento XVI, que tinha sido eleito cinco anos antes. "Essa foi boa?" Outra abanar do dedo. "Eu não gosto muito dele. Ele não tem a idéia certa. Assim que eu tenho tempo, eu quero organizar uma greve por todas as mulheres aa Igreja, em todo o mundo. A igreja não funciona sem as mulheres. Nós podemos fazê-lo parar até que o papa reorganiza as regras. Devagar aqui em frente... "

Eu deacelero numa curva descendente. Os faróis de iluminam um conjunto de cruzes de madeira e flores de plástico no banco. Leonora toca a testa e ambos os lados de seu peito e diz: "Um monte de gente morram aqui."

Estamos em silêncio por um tempo. Estou pensando em caminhoneiros bêbados e famílias embalados em motocicletas. Ela ainda está pensando sobre a Igreja.

"Alguns dos bispos nos ajudaram", diz ela, "mas a maioria não. Eles só querem dinheiro. "

E lá estão eles novamente: os ricos. A classe alta, a vaca leiteira, que a Igreja tem sido ordenhando desde os tempos coloniais, não quer ver a mudança, diz ela. Eles querem que o clero se ater ao Evangelho e ficar de fora da política. Ela está decepcionada com o falta da Igreja a utilizar o seu poder global para derrubar tiranos, forçar corporações a se submeter, efetuar a distribuição justa da terra, e prevenir a civilização de exterminar-se. Isto é, evidentemente, uma tarefa difícil. Mas Leonora ajusta suas vistas alta, e não mostra indicação nenhuma de se esgotar.

"Eu poderia estar em paz", diz ela. "Eu poderia me aposentar, ter uma vida mais tranquila. Mas é impossível ficar tranquilo quando vejo os meus irmãos, os seres humanos, sofrer. Impossível. "

Quase três anos depois, a tranquilidade parece longe perto do que nunca, com os poderosos e os humildes ainda travado na sua cabo-de-guerra contínua. Elizete Pinheiro foi demitida de seu emprego na prefeitura de Terra Nova do Norte por seu envolvimento em causas de justiça social e campanhas de conservação. Um mandado foi emitido para a prisão de Sebastião Neves de Almeida sob várias acusações, mas ele ainda estava livre e sem fazer nenhum esforço para se esconder. Cinco fazendas foram pegos utilizando trabalho escravo. Um avião de pulverização lançou algo tóxico nas casas e jardins do acampamento Renascer, matando culturas e enviando as pessoas para o hospital, e alguém deu tiros numa casa ocupada por crianças e idosos. Uma bomba explodiu debaixo do pneu do carro de Leonora. E enquanto o Senado brasileiro debateu (e, eventualmente, passou) uma nova lei que permite aumento significativo do desmatamento, Leonora e ativistas de todo o país foram recheados com ameaças de morte. Um padre ao norte da Terra Nova recebeu vários, mas Leonora, em que tem de ser visto como um sinal de progresso, recebeu apenas uma.

If you found this book interesting, you might
be interested in another book in the same
series, *Love and Death in the Kingdom of Swaziland.* It's about two Cabrini sisters working
in the outback of southern Africa, where one in
three people has HIV, lethal snakes run ram-
pant, children run households, orphans wander
without even the most distant living relative,
and a king ignores the imminent extinction of
his kingdom. You can read excerpts and see
photos at cheneybooks.com . It's available in
print and in an eBook edition for iPad, Kobo,
Kindle, and Nook.

Glenn Alan Cheney

Acknowledgement

I would like to thank the many people who made this
book possible and helped me get into and out of Mato
Grosso. Obviously Sister Leonora and the many people
named in this book provided a great deal of information
and care. Among those not mentioned are Norma, Mariza, Ivaine, Bete, Evenaldo, and Teobaldo. I thank the
folks at the Hotel Avenida — Nêgo, Ingrid, Ana Beatriz,
and Marianne — for making their hotel a home. I thank
the folks at the *acampamentos* — those mentioned in
this book, and so many others — for their openness,
courage, kindness, and generosity. I offer especially
deep thanks to the Pinheiro family — Maria Elizete,
Tcharlim, Vanessa, Valquiria, Paulo, and the rest of the
clan — for taking me into their fold and teaching me
so much. I am indebted to James Marcus for his kind
guidance in getting this complicated story to a size and
tone appropriate for *Harper's*. Photographer Nadia Shira
Cohen was a big help in finding last-minute details.
Thanks, too, to Elisabete dos Santos and Luciana Tanure
for help with translation. Denise Dembinski gets credit
for proof-reading. And extra special thanks go to my
wife, Solange Aurora, for her patience, support, and
encouragement.

Glenn Alan Cheney

The Author

Glenn Alan Cheney is the author of more than 20 books, hundreds of articles, and many an op-ed essay. His books, fiction and nonfiction for children, teens, and adults, are on such disparate topics as nuclear proliferation, Mohandas Gandhi, Abraham Lincoln, atomic testing, television, Central American politics, the Pilgrims, Brazil, and Chernobyl. Most of his articles are about business, finance, and accounting. The *Harper's* article about sister Leonora and this book are part of a book he is writing about sisters who work under difficult or dangerous conditions. (*Love and Death in the Kingdom of Swaziland* is another part of that book.) He holds degrees in philosophy, communication, English, and creative writing. Active in local politics, he has served on his town's board of selectmen, board of finance, inland wetlands commission, volunteer fire department, library board, and historical society. He lives in Hanover, Conn., with his wife, Solange.

Made in the USA
Charleston, SC
28 December 2013